P9-APH-625

MONTGOMERY COLLEGE LIBRARY
GERMANTOWN CAMPUS

# 100 More Story Poems

# 100 More
# Story Poems

SELECTED BY ELINOR PARKER

ILLUSTRATED BY PETER SPIER

Thomas Y. Crowell Company

New York

### By Elinor Parker

100 STORY POEMS

MOST GRACIOUS MAJESTY

100 POEMS ABOUT PEOPLE

I WAS JUST THINKING

100 MORE STORY POEMS

THE SINGING AND THE GOLD

POEMS OF WILLIAM WORDSWORTH

*Copyright © 1960 by Elinor Parker*
*All rights reserved. No part of this book*
*may be reproduced in any form, except by a reviewer,*
*without the permission of the publisher.*
*Manufactured in the United States of America*

*Library of Congress Catalog Card No. 60-11543*
*ISBN 0-690-59690-1*

*9 10 11 12 13 14 15*

For permission to reprint the copyrighted poems in this anthology, acknowledgment is extended to the following:

Appleton-Century-Crofts, Inc., for "The Elf and the Dormouse" by Oliver Herford from *St. Nicholas Book of Verse*. Copyright, 1923, the Century Company.

Mrs. George Bambridge, Doubleday & Company, Inc., and the Macmillan Company of Canada, Ltd., for "Cold Iron" from *Rewards and Fairies* by Rudyard Kipling and "The Land" from *A Diversity of Creatures* by Rudyard Kipling.

Beatrice Curtis Brown for "Jonathan Bing," copyright © 1936 by Beatrice Curtis Brown.

Mrs. James Branch Cabell for "Story of the Flowery Kingdom" by James Branch Cabell.

Houghton Mifflin Company for "Patterns" by Amy Lowell from *The Complete Poetical Works of Amy Lowell*.

Bruce Humphries, Inc., for "Babushka" from *The Children of Christmas* by Edith M. Thomas.

Alfred A. Knopf, Inc., for "Matilda, Who Told Lies and Was Burned to Death" from *Cautionary Verses* by Hilaire Belloc, copyright 1931 by Hilaire Belloc.

J. B. Lippincott Company for "Forty Singing Seamen" and "The River of Stars" from *Collected Poems*, volume 1 and volume 3, by Alfred Noyes, copyright 1906, 1934 by Alfred Noyes.

Little, Brown & Company for "The Adventures of Isabel" by Ogden Nash.

Macmillan & Co., Ltd., and Wilfrid Gibson for "The Dancing Seal" by Wilfrid Gibson.

The Macmillan Company for "Eve" from *Collected Poems* by Ralph Hodgson and "Spanish Waters" from *Collected Poems* by John Masefield.

William Morrow and Company, Inc., for "How I Brought the Good News from Aix to Ghent" from *Horse Nonsense* by R. J. Yeatman and W. C. Sellar, copyright 1934 by William Morrow and Company, Inc.

Charles Scribner's Sons for "Ballad of the Golden Bowl" from *The Delicate Balance* by Sara Henderson Hay, copyright 1951 Charles Scribner's Sons.

Edward W. Stitt, Jr., for "The Horse Thief" by William Rose Benét.

Louis Untermeyer for "The Butterfly and the Caterpillar" by Joseph Lauren.

# Contents

# Contents

# Just for Fun

# The Three Huntsmen

There were three jovial Welshmen,
    As I have heard them say,
And they would go a-hunting, boys,
    Upon St. David's Day.
All the day they hunted,
    And nothing could they find,
But a ship a-sailing,
    A-sailing with the wind.
        And a-hunting they did go.

One said it was a ship,
    The other he said, Nay;
The third said it was a house
    With the chimney blown away.
And all the night they hunted,
    And nothing could they find,
But the moon a-gliding,
    A-gliding with the wind.
        And a-hunting they did go.

One said it was the moon,
    The other he said, Nay;
The third said it was a cheese
    And half o't cut away.

And all the day they hunted,
　And nothing could they find,
But a hedgehog in a bramble bush,
　And that they left behind.
　　And a-hunting they did go.

The first said it was a hedgehog,
　The second he said, Nay;
The third, it was a pincushion,
　The pins stuck in wrong way.
And all the night they hunted,
　And nothing could they find,
But a hare in a turnip field,
　And that they left behind.
　　And a-hunting they did go.

The first said it was a hare,
　The second he said, Nay;
The third, he said it was a calf,
　And the cow had run away.
And all the day they hunted,
　And nothing could they find,
But an owl in a holly-tree
　And that they left behind.
　　And a-hunting they did go.

One said it was an owl,
　The second he said, Nay;
The third said 'twas an old man
　And his beard growing grey.

3

Then all three jovial Welshmen
Came riding home at last,
'For three days we have nothing killed,
And never broke our fast!'
And a-hunting they did go.

*Traditional: English*

# A Strange Story

There was an old woman, as I've heard tell,
She went to market her eggs to sell;
She went to market all on a market-day,
And she fell asleep on the king's highway.

There came by a peddler whose name was Stout;
He cut her petticoats all round about;
He cut her petticoats up to the knees,
Which made the old woman to shiver and freeze.

When this little woman first did wake,
She began to shiver and she began to shake;
She began to wonder and she began to cry,
"Oh! deary, deary me, this is none of I!

"But if it be I, as I do hope it be,
I've a little dog at home, and he'll know me;
If it be I, he'll wag his little tail,
And if it be not I, he'll loudly bark and wail."

Home went the little woman all in the dark;
Up got the little dog, and he began to bark;
He began to bark, so she began to cry,
"Oh! deary, deary me, this is none of I!"

*Old Rhyme*

5

# Matilda

WHO TOLD LIES, AND WAS BURNED TO DEATH

Matilda told such Dreadful Lies
It made one Gasp and Stretch one's Eyes;
Her Aunt, who from her Earliest Youth,
Had kept a Strict Regard for Truth,
Attempted to Believe Matilda:
The effort very nearly killed her,
And would have done so, had not She
Discovered this Infirmity.
For once, towards the Close of Day,
Matilda, growing tired of play,
And finding she was left alone,
Went tiptoe to the Telephone
And summoned the Immediate Aid
Of London's Noble Fire-Brigade.
Within an hour the Gallant Band
Were pouring in on every hand,
From Putney, Hackney Downs and Bow,
With Courage high and Hearts a-glow
They galloped, roaring through the Town,
"Matilda's House is Burning Down!"

Inspired by British Cheers and Loud
Proceeding from the Frenzied Crowd,

6

They ran their ladders through a score
Of windows on the Ball Room Floor.
And took Peculiar Pains to Souse
The Pictures up and down the House
Until Matilda's Aunt succeeded
In showing them they were not needed
And even then she had to pay
To get the Men to go away!

\*   \*   \*   \*   \*

It happened that a few Weeks later
Her Aunt was off to the Theatre
To see that Interesting Play
*The Second Mrs. Tanqueray.*
She had refused to take her Niece
To hear this Entertaining Piece:
A Deprivation Just and Wise
To Punish her for Telling Lies.
That Night a Fire *did* break out—
You should have heard Matilda Shout!
You should have heard her Scream and Bawl,
And throw the window up and call
To People passing in the Street—
(The rapidly increasing Heat
Encouraging her to obtain
Their confidence)—but all in vain!
For every time She shouted "Fire!"
They only answered "Little Liar!"
And therefore when her Aunt returned
Matilda, and the House, were Burned.

*Hilaire Belloc*

# Jonathan Bing

Poor old Jonathan Bing
Went out in his carriage to visit the King,
But everyone pointed and said, "Look at that!
Jonathan Bing has forgotten his hat!"
(He'd forgotten his hat!)

Poor old Jonathan Bing
Went home and put on a new hat for the King,
But up by the palace a soldier said, "Hi!
You can't see the King; you've forgotten your tie!"
(He'd forgotten his tie!)

Poor old Jonathan Bing,
He put on a *beautiful* tie for the King,
But when he arrived an Archbishop said, "Ho!
You can't come to court in pyjamas, you know!"

Poor old Jonathan Bing
Went home and addressed a short note to the King:
   If you please will excuse me
   I won't come to tea;
   For home's the best place for
   All people like me!

*Beatrice Curtis Brown*

# Story of the Flowery Kingdom

*"La belle Sou-Chong-Thé, au claire de pleine Lune."*—Paul Verville

Fair Sou-Chong-Tee, by a shimmering brook
Where ghost-like lilies loomed tall and straight,
Met young Too-Hi, in a moonlit nook,
Where they cooed and kissed till the hour was late:
Then, with lanterns, a mandarin passed in state,
Named Hoo-Hung-Hoo of the Golden Band,
Who had wooed the maiden to be *his* mate,—
For these things occur in the Flowery Land.

Now, Hoo-Hung-Hoo had written a book,
In seven volumes, to celebrate
The death of the Emperor's thirteenth cook:
So, being a person whose power was great,
He ordered a herald to indicate
He would blind Too-Hi with a red-hot brand
And marry Sou-Chong at a quarter-past eight,—
For these things occur in the Flowery Land.

Whilst the brand was heating, the lovers shook
In their several shoes,—when by lucky fate
A Dragon came, with his tail in a crook,—
A Dragon out of a Nankeen Plate,—

9

And gobbled the hard-hearted potentate
And all of his servants, and snorted, *and*
Passed on at a super-cyclonic rate,—
For these things occur in the Flowery Land.

The lovers were wed at an early date,
And lived for the future, I understand,
In one continuous tête-à-tête,—
For these things occur . . . in the Flowery Land.

*James Branch Cabell*

# Humpty Dumpty's Song

In winter, when the fields are white,
I sing this song for your delight—

In spring, when woods are getting green,
I'll try and tell you what I mean:

In summer, when the days are long,
Perhaps you'll understand the song:

In autumn, when the leaves are brown,
Take pen and ink, and write it down.

I sent a message to the fish:
I told them "This is what I wish."

The little fishes of the sea,
They sent an answer back to me.

The little fishes' answer was
"We cannot do it, Sir, because—"

I sent to them again to say
"It will be better to obey."

The fishes answered, with a grin,
"Why, what a temper you are in!"

I told them once, I told them twice:
They would not listen to advice.

I took a kettle large and new,
Fit for the deed I had to do.

My heart went hop, my heart went thump:
I filled the kettle at the pump.

Then some one came to me and said
"The little fishes are in bed."

I said to him, I said it plain,
"Then you must wake them up again."

I said it very loud and clear:
I went and shouted in his ear.

But he was very stiff and proud:
He said, "You needn't shout so loud!"

And he was very proud and stiff:
He said: "I'd go and wake them, if—"

I took a corkscrew from the shelf:
I went to wake them up myself.

And when I found the door was locked,
I pulled and pushed and kicked and knocked.

And when I found the door was shut,
I tried to turn the handle, but—

There was a long pause.
"Is that all?" Alice timidly asked.
"That's all," said Humpty Dumpty. "Good-bye."

*Lewis Carroll*

# The Hunting of the Snark

"Just the place for a Snark!" the Bellman cried
    As he landed his crew with care;
Supporting each man on the top of the tide
    By a finger entwined in his hair.

"Just the place for a Snark! I have said it twice:
    That alone should encourage the crew.
Just the place for a Snark! I have said it thrice:
    What I tell you three times is true."

The crew was complete: it included a Boots—
    A maker of Bonnets and Hoods—
A Barrister, brought to arrange their disputes—
    And a Broker, to value their goods.

A Billiard-marker, whose skill was immense,
    Might perhaps have won more than his share—
But a Banker, engaged at enormous expense,
    Had the whole of their cash in his care.

There was also a Beaver, that paced on the deck,
    Or would sit making lace in the bow:

And had often (the Bellman said) saved them from wreck
    Though none of the sailors knew how.

There was one who was famed for the number of things
    He forgot when he entered the ship:
His umbrella, his watch, all his jewels and rings,
    And the clothes he had bought for the trip.

He had forty-two boxes, all carefully packed,
    With his name painted clearly on each:
But, since he omitted to mention the fact,
    They were all left behind on the beach.

The loss of his clothes hardly mattered, because
    He had seven coats on when he came,
With three pair of boots—but the worst of it was,
    He had wholly forgotten his name.

He would answer to "Hi!" or to any loud cry,
    Such as "Fry me!" or "Fritter my wig!"
To "What-you-may-call-um!" or "What-was-his-name!"
    But especially "Thing-um-a-jig!"

While, for those who preferred a more forcible word,
    He had different names from these:
His intimate friends called him "Candle-ends,"
    And his enemies "Toasted-cheese."

"His form is ungainly—his intellect small—"
    (So the Bellman would often remark)—
"But his courage is perfect! And that, after all,
    Is the thing that one needs with a Snark."

15

He would joke with hyænas, returning their stare
    With an impudent wag of the head:
And he once went a walk, paw-in-paw, with a bear,
    "Just to keep up its spirits," he said.

He came as a Baker: but owned, when too late—
    And it drove the poor Bellman half-mad—
He could only bake Bride-cake—for which, I may state,
    No materials were to be had.

The last of the crew needs especial remark,
    Though he looked an incredible dunce:
He had just one idea—but, that one being "Snark,"
    The good Bellman engaged him at once.

He came as a Butcher: but gravely declared,
    When the ship had been sailing a week,
He could only kill Beavers. The Bellman looked scared,
    And was almost too frightened to speak:

But at length he explained, in a tremulous tone,
    There was only one Beaver on board;
And that was a tame one he had of his own,
    Whose death would be deeply deplored.

The Beaver, who happened to hear the remark,
    Protested, with tears in its eyes,
That not even the rapture of hunting the Snark
    Could atone for that dismal surprise!

It strongly advised that the Butcher should be
    Conveyed in a separate ship:

16

But the Bellman declared that would never agree
 With the plans he had made for the trip:

Navigation was always a difficult art,
 Though with only one ship and one bell:
And he feared he must really decline, for his part,
 Undertaking another as well.

The Beaver's best course was, no doubt, to procure
 A second-hand dagger-proof coat—
So the Baker advised it—and next, to insure
 Its life in some Office of note:

This the Banker suggested, and offered for hire
 (On moderate terms), or for sale,
Two excellent Policies, one Against Fire
 And one Against Damage From Hail.

Yet still, ever after that sorrowful day,
 Whenever the Butcher was by,
The Beaver kept looking the opposite way,
 And appeared unaccountably shy.


FIT THE SECOND
THE BELLMAN'S SPEECH


The Bellman himself they all praised to the skies—
 Such a carriage, such ease and such grace!
Such solemnity, too! One could see he was wise,
 The moment one looked in his face!

17

He had bought a large map representing the sea,
  Without the least vestige of land:
And the crew were much pleased when they found it to be
  A map they could all understand.

"What's the good of Mercator's North Poles and Equators,
  Tropics, Zones, and Meridian Lines?"
So the Bellman would cry: and the crew would reply
  "They are merely conventional signs!

"Other maps are such shapes, with their islands and capes!
  But we've got our brave Captain to thank"
(So the crew would protest) "that he's bought *us* the
      best—
  A perfect and absolute blank!"

This was charming, no doubt: but they shortly found out
  That the Captain they trusted so well
Had only one notion for crossing the ocean,
  And that was to tingle his bell.

He was thoughtful and grave—but the orders he gave
  Were enough to bewilder a crew.
When he cried "Steer to starboard, but keep her head
      larboard!"
  What on earth was the helmsman to do?

Then the bowsprit got mixed with the rudder sometimes:
  A thing, as the Bellman remarked,
That frequently happens in tropical climes,
  When a vessel is, so to speak, "snarked."

But the principal failing occurred in the sailing,
  And the Bellman, perplexed and distressed,
Said he *had* hoped, at least, when the wind blew due East,
  That the ship would *not* travel due West!

But the danger was past—they had landed at last,
  With their boxes, portmanteaus, and bags:
Yet at first sight the crew were not pleased with the view
  Which consisted of chasms and crags.

The Bellman perceived that their spirits were low,
  And repeated in musical tone
Some jokes he had kept for a season of woe—
  But the crew would do nothing but groan.

He served out some grog with a liberal hand,
  And bade them sit down on the beach:
And they could not but own that their Captain looked
    grand,
  As he stood and delivered his speech.

"Friends, Romans, and countrymen, lend me your ears!"
  (They were all of them fond of quotations:
So they drank to his health, and they gave him three
    cheers,
  While he served out additional rations).

"We have sailed many months, we have sailed many
    weeks,
  (Four weeks to the month you may mark),
But never as yet ('tis your Captain who speaks)
  Have we caught the least glimpse of a Snark!

"We have sailed many weeks, we have sailed many days,
 (Seven days to the week I allow),
But a Snark, on the which we might lovingly gaze,
 We have never beheld till now!

"Come, listen, my men, while I tell you again
 The five unmistakable marks
By which you may know, wheresoever you go,
 The warranted genuine Snarks.

"Let us take them in order. The first is the taste,
 Which is meagre and hollow, but crisp:
Like a coat that is rather too tight in the waist,
 With a flavour of Will-o'-the-Wisp.

"Its habit of getting up late you'll agree
 That it carries too far, when I say
That it frequently breakfasts at five-o'clock tea,
 And dines on the following day.

"The third is its slowness in taking a jest.
 Should you happen to venture on one,
It will sigh like a thing that is deeply distressed:
 And it always looks grave at a pun.

"The fourth is its fondness for bathing-machines,
 Which it constantly carries about,
And believes that they add to the beauty of scenes—
 A sentiment open to doubt.

"The fifth is ambition. It next will be right
 To describe each particular batch:

Distinguishing those that have feathers, and bite,
From those that have whiskers, and scratch.

"For, although common Snarks do no manner of harm,
Yet I feel it my duty to say
Some are Boojums—" The Bellman broke off in alarm,
For the Baker had fainted away.

### FIT THE THIRD
#### THE BAKER'S TALE

They roused him with muffins—they roused him with
ice—
They roused him with mustard and cress—
They roused him with jam and judicious advice—
They set him conundrums to guess.

When at length he sat up and was able to speak,
His sad story he offered to tell;
And the Bellman cried "Silence! Not even a shriek!"
And excitedly tingled his bell.

There was silence supreme! Not a shriek, not a scream,
Scarcely even a howl or a groan,
As the man they called "Ho!" told his story of woe
In an antediluvian tone.

"My father and mother were honest, though poor—"
"Skip all that!" cried the Bellman in haste.
"If it once becomes dark, there's no chance of a Snark—
We have hardly a minute to waste!"

"I skip forty years," said the Baker in tears,
  "And proceed without further remark
To the day when you took me aboard of your ship
  To help you in hunting the Snark.

"A dear uncle of mine (after whom I was named)
  Remarked, when I bade him farewell—"
"Oh, skip your dear uncle!" the Bellman exclaimed,
  As he angrily tingled his bell.

"He remarked to me then," said that mildest of men,
  " 'If your Snark be a Snark, that is right:
Fetch it home by all means—you may serve it with greens
  And it's handy for striking a light.

" 'You may seek it with thimbles—and seek it with care;
  You may hunt it with forks and hope;
You may threaten its life with a railway-share;
  You may charm it with smiles and soap—' "

("That's exactly the method," the Bellman bold
  In a hasty parenthesis cried,
"That's exactly the way I have always been told
  That the capture of Snarks should be tried!")

" 'But oh, beamish nephew, beware of the day,
  If your Snark be a Boojum! For then
You will softly and suddenly vanish away,
  And never be met with again!'

"It is this, it is this that oppresses my soul,
  When I think of my uncle's last words:

22

And my heart is like nothing so much as a bowl
   Brimming over with quivering curds!

"It is this, it is this—" "We have had that before!"
   The Bellman indignantly said.
And the Baker replied "Let me say it once more.
   It is this, it is this that I dread!

"I engage with the Snark—every night after dark—
   In a dreamy delirious fight:
I serve it with greens in those shadowy scenes,
   And I use it for striking a light:

"But if ever I meet with a Boojum, that day,
   In a moment (of this I am sure),
I shall softly and suddenly vanish away—
   And the notion I cannot endure!"

FIT THE FOURTH

THE HUNTING

The Bellman looked uffish, and wrinkled his brow.
   "If only you'd spoken before!
It's excessively awkward to mention it now,
   With the Snark, so to speak, at the door!

"We should all of us grieve, as you well may believe,
   If you never were met with again—
But surely, my man, when the voyage began,
   You might have suggested it then?

23

"It's excessively awkward to mention it now—
  As I think I've already remarked."
And the man they called "Hi!" replied, with a sigh,
  "I informed you the day we embarked.


"You may charge me with murder—or want of sense—
  (We are all of us weak at times):
But the slightest approach to a false pretence
  Was never among my crimes!


"I said it in Hebrew—I said it in Dutch—
  I said it in German and Greek:
But I wholly forgot (and it vexes me much)
  That English is what you speak!"


" 'Tis a pitiful tale," said the Bellman, whose face
  Had grown longer at every word:
"But, now that you've stated the whole of your case,
  More debate would be simply absurd.


"The rest of my speech" (he exclaimed to his men)
  "You shall hear when I've leisure to speak it.
But the Snark is at hand, let me tell you again!
  'Tis your glorious duty to seek it!


"To seek it with thimbles, to seek it with care;
  To pursue it with forks and hope;
To threaten its life with a railway-share;
  To charm it with smiles and soap!

"For the Snark's a peculiar creature, that won't
   Be caught in a commonplace way.
Do all that you know, and try all that you don't:
   Not a chance must be wasted to-day!

"For England expects—I forbear to proceed:
   'Tis a maxim tremendous, but trite:
And you'd best be unpacking the things that you need
   To rig yourselves out for the fight."

Then the Banker endorsed a blank cheque (which he
      crossed),
   And changed his loose silver for notes:
The Baker with care combed his whiskers and hair,
   And shook the dust out of his coats.

The Boots and the Broker were sharpening a spade—
   Each working the grindstone in turn:
But the Beaver went on making lace, and displayed
   No interest in the concern:

Though the Barrister tried to appeal to its pride,
   And vainly proceeded to cite
A number of cases, in which making laces
   Had been proved an infringement of right.

The maker of Bonnets ferociously planned
   A novel arrangement of bows:
While the Billiard-marker with quivering hand
   Was chalking the tip of his nose.

But the Butcher turned nervous, and dressed himself fine,
  With yellow kid gloves and a ruff—
Said he felt it exactly like going to dine,
  Which the Bellman declared was all "stuff."

"Introduce me, now there's a good fellow," he said,
  "If we happen to meet it together!"
And the Bellman, sagaciously nodding his head,
  Said "That must depend on the weather."

The Beaver went simply galumphing about,
  At seeing the Butcher so shy:
And even the Baker, though stupid and stout,
  Made an effort to wink with one eye.

"Be a man!" cried the Bellman in wrath, as he heard
  The Butcher beginning to sob.
"Should we meet with a Jubjub, that desperate bird,
  We shall need all our strength for the job!"

#### FIT THE FIFTH
#### THE BEAVER'S LESSON

They sought it with thimbles, they sought it with care;
  They pursued it with forks and hope;
They threatened its life with a railway-share;
  They charmed it with smiles and soap.

Then the Butcher contrived an ingenious plan
  For making a separate sally;
And had fixed on a spot unfrequented by man,
  A dismal and desolate valley.

But the very same plan to the Beaver occurred:
    It had chosen the very same place:
Yet neither betrayed, by a sign or a word,
    The disgust that appeared in his face.


Each thought he was thinking of nothing but "Snark"
    And the glorious work of the day;
And each tried to pretend that he did not remark
    That the other was going that way.


But the valley grew narrow and narrower still,
    And the evening got darker and colder,
Till (merely from nervousness, not from good will)
    They marched along shoulder to shoulder.


Then a scream, shrill and high, rent the shuddering sky
    And they knew that some danger was near:
The Beaver turned pale to the tip of its tail,
    And even the Butcher felt queer.


He thought of his childhood, left far behind—
    That blissful and innocent state—
The sound so exactly recalled to his mind
    A pencil that squeaks on a slate!


" 'Tis the voice of the Jubjub!" he suddenly cried.
    (This man, that they used to call "Dunce.")
"As the Bellman would tell you," he added with pride,
    "I have uttered that sentiment once.

" 'Tis the note of the Jubjub! Keep count, I entreat.
    You will find I have told it you twice.
'Tis the song of the Jubjub! The proof is complete.
    If only I've stated it thrice."

The Beaver had counted with scrupulous care,
    Attending to every word:
But it fairly lost heart, and outgrabe in despair,
    When the third repetition occurred.

It felt that, in spite of all possible pains,
    It had somehow contrived to lose count,
And the only thing now was to rack its poor brains
    By reckoning up the amount.

"Two added to one—if that could but be done,"
    It said, "with one's fingers and thumbs!"
Recollecting with tears how, in earlier years,
    It had taken no pains with its sums.

"The thing can be done," said the Butcher, "I think
    The thing must be done, I am sure.
The thing shall be done! Bring me paper and ink,
    The best there is time to procure."

The Beaver brought paper, portfolio, pens,
    And ink in unfailing supplies:
While strange creepy creatures came out of their dens,
    And watched them with wondering eyes.

So engrossed was the Butcher, he heeded them not,
  As he wrote with a pen in each hand,
And explained all the while in a popular style
  Which the Beaver could well understand.

"Taking Three as the subject to reason about—
  A convenient number to state—
We add Seven, and Ten, and then multiply out
  By One Thousand diminished by Eight.

"The result we proceed to divide, as you see,
  By Nine Hundred and Ninety and Two;
Then subtract Seventeen, and the answer must be
  Exactly and perfectly true.

"The method employed I would gladly explain,
  While I have it so clear in my head,
If I had but the time and you had but the brain—
  But much yet remains to be said.

"In one moment I've seen what has hitherto been
  Enveloped in absolute mystery,
And without extra charge I will give you at large
  A Lesson in Natural History."

In his genial way he proceeded to say
  (Forgetting all laws of propriety,
And that giving instruction, without introduction,
  Would have caused quite a thrill in Society),

"As to temper the Jubjub's a desperate bird.
  Since it lives in perpetual passion:
Its taste in costume is entirely absurd—
  It is ages ahead of the fashion:

"But it knows any friend it has met once before:
  It never will look at a bribe:
And in charity-meetings it stands at the door,
  And collects—though it does not subscribe.

"Its flavour when cooked is more exquisite far
  Than mutton, or oysters, or eggs:
(Some think it keeps best in an ivory jar,
  And some, in mahogany kegs:)

"You boil it in sawdust: you salt it in glue:
  You condense it with locusts and tape:
Still keeping one principal object in view—
  To preserve its symmetrical shape."

The Butcher would gladly have talked till next day,
  But he felt that the Lesson must end,
And he wept with delight in attempting to say
  He considered the Beaver his friend:

While the Beaver confessed, with affectionate looks
  More eloquent even than tears,
It had learned in ten minutes far more than all books
  Would have taught it in seventy years.

They returned hand-in-hand, and the Bellman, un-
  manned
  (For a moment) with noble emotion,
Said "This amply repays all the wearisome days
  We have spent on the billowy ocean!"


Such friends, as the Beaver and Butcher became,
  Have seldom if ever been known;
In winter or summer, 'twas always the same—
  You could never meet either alone.


And when quarrels arose—as one frequently finds
  Quarrels will, spite of every endeavour—
The song of the Jubjub recurred to their minds,
  And cemented their friendship for ever!


FIT THE SIXTH
THE BARRISTER'S DREAM


They sought it with thimbles, they sought it with care;
  They pursued it with forks and hope;
They threatened its life with a railway-share;
  They charmed it with smiles and soap.


But the Barrister, weary of proving in vain
  That the Beaver's lace-making was wrong,
Fell asleep, and in dreams saw the creature quite plain
  That his fancy had dwelt on so long.

31

He dreamed that he stood in a shadowy Court,
  Where the Snark, with a glass in its eye,
Dressed in gown, bands, and wig, was defending a pig
  On the charge of deserting its sty.

The Witnesses proved, without error or flaw,
  That the sty was deserted when found:
And the Judge kept explaining the state of the law
  In a soft under-current of sound.

The indictment had never been clearly expressed,
  And it seemed that the Snark had begun,
And had spoken three hours, before any one guessed
  What the pig was supposed to have done.

The Jury had each formed a different view
  (Long before the indictment was read),
And they all spoke at once, so that none of them knew
  One word that the others had said.

"You must know—" said the Judge: but the Snark ex-
      claimed "Fudge!
  That statute is obsolete quite!
Let me tell you, my friends, the whole question depends
  On an ancient manorial right.

"In the matter of Treason the pig would appear
  To have aided, but scarcely abetted:
While the charge of Insolvency fails, it is clear,
  If you grant the plea 'never indebted.'

32

"The fact of Desertion I will not dispute:
   But its guilt, as I trust, is removed
(So far as relates to the costs of this suit)
   By the Alibi which has been proved.

"My poor client's fate now depends on your votes."
   Here the speaker sat down in his place,
And directed the Judge to refer to his notes
   And briefly to sum up the case.

But the Judge said he never had summed up before;
   So the Snark undertook it instead,
And summed it so well that it came to far more
   Than the Witnesses ever had said!

When the verdict was called for, the Jury declined,
   As the word was so puzzling to spell;
But they ventured to hope that the Snark wouldn't mind
   Undertaking that duty as well.

So the Snark found the verdict, although, as it owned,
   It was spent with the toils of the day:
When it said the word "GUILTY!" the Jury all groaned
   And some of them fainted away.

Then the Snark pronounced sentence, the Judge being
      quite
   Too nervous to utter a word:
When it rose to its feet, there was silence like night,
   And the fall of a pin might be heard.

"Transportation for life" was the sentence it gave,
  "And *then* to be fined forty pound."
The Jury all cheered, though the Judge said he feared
  That the phrase was not legally sound.

But their wild exultation was suddenly checked
  When the jailer informed them, with tears,
Such a sentence would have not the slightest effect,
  As the pig had been dead for some years.

The Judge left the Court, looking deeply disgusted
  But the Snark, though a little aghast,
As the lawyer to whom the defence was intrusted,
  Went bellowing on to the last.

Thus the Barrister dreamed, while the bellowing seemed
  To grow every moment more clear:
Till he woke to the knell of a furious bell,
  Which the Bellman rang close at his ear.

### FIT THE SEVENTH
#### THE BANKER'S FATE

They sought it with thimbles, they sought it with care;
  They pursued it with forks and hope;
They threatened its life with a railway-share;
  They charmed it with smiles and soap.

And the Banker, inspired with a courage so new
  It was matter for general remark,
Rushed madly ahead and was lost to their view
  In his zeal to discover the Snark.

34

But while he was seeking with thimbles and care,
  A Bandersnatch swiftly drew nigh
And grabbed at the Banker, who shrieked in despair,
  For he knew it was useless to fly.

He offered large discount—he offered a cheque
  (Drawn "to bearer") for seven-pounds-ten:
But the Bandersnatch merely extended its neck
  And grabbed at the Banker again.

Without rest or pause—while those frumious jaws
  Went savagely snapping around—
He skipped and he hopped, and he floundered and
      flopped,
  Till fainting he fell to the ground.

The Bandersnatch fled as the others appeared
  Led on by that fear-stricken yell:
And the Bellman remarked "It is just as I feared!"
  And solemnly tolled on his bell.

He was black in the face, and they scarcely could trace
  The least likeness to what he had been:
While so great was his fright that his waistcoat turned
      white—
  A wonderful thing to be seen!

To the horror of all who were present that day,
  He uprose in full evening dress,
And with senseless grimaces endeavoured to say
  What his tongue could no longer express.

Down he sank in a chair—ran his hands through his
    hair—
And chanted in mimsiest tones
Words whose utter inanity proved his insanity,
    While he rattled a couple of bones.

"Leave him here to his fate—it is getting so late!"
    The Bellman exclaimed in a fright.
"We have lost half the day. Any further delay,
    And we shan't catch a Snark before night!"

### FIT THE EIGHTH
#### THE VANISHING

They sought it with thimbles, they sought it with care;
    They pursued it with forks and hope;
They threatened its life with a railway-share;
    They charmed it with smiles and soap.

They shuddered to think that the chase might fail,
    And the Beaver, excited at last,
Went bounding along on the tip of its tail,
    For the daylight was nearly past.

"There is Thingumbob shouting!" the Bellman said.
    "He is shouting like mad, only hark!
He is waving his hands, he is wagging his head,
    He has certainly found a Snark!"

They gazed in delight, while the Butcher exclaimed
    "He was always a desperate wag!"

36

They beheld him—their Baker—their hero unnamed—
  On the top of a neighbouring crag,

Erect and sublime, for one moment of time
  In the next, that wild figure they saw
(As if stung by a spasm) plunge into a chasm,
  While they waited and listened in awe.

"It's a Snark!" was the sound that first came to their ears,
  And seemed almost too good to be true.
Then followed a torrent of laughter and cheers:
  Then the ominous words "It's a Boo—"

Then, silence. Some fancied they heard in the air
  A weary and wandering sigh
That sounded like "—jum!" but the others declare
  It was only a breeze that went by.

They hunted till darkness came on, but they found
  Not a button, or feather, or mark,
By which they could tell that they stood on the ground
  Where the Baker had met with the Snark.

In the midst of the word he was trying to say,
  In the midst of his laughter and glee,
He had softly and suddenly vanished away—
  For the Snark *was* a Boojum, you see.

*Lewis Carroll*

# The Embarrassing Episode of Little Miss Muffet

Little Miss Muffet discovered a tuffet,
    (Which never occurred to the rest of us)
And, as 'twas a June day, and just about noonday,
    She wanted to eat—like the best of us:
Her diet was whey, and I hasten to say
    It is wholesome and people grow fat on it.
The spot being lonely, the lady not only
    Discovered the tuffet, but sat on it.

A rivulet gabbled beside her and babbled,
    As rivulets always are thought to do,
And dragon flies sported around and cavorted,
    As poets say dragon flies ought to do;
When, glancing aside for a moment, she spied
    A horrible sight that brought fear to her,
A hideous spider was sitting beside her,
    And most unavoidably near to her!

Albeit unsightly, this creature politely
    Said: "Madam, I earnestly vow to you,
I'm penitent that I did not bring my hat. I
    Should otherwise certainly bow to you."

Though anxious to please, he was so ill at ease
    That he lost all his sense of propriety,
And grew so inept that he clumsily stept
    In her plate—which is barred in Society.

This curious error completed her terror;
    She shuddered, and growing much paler, not
Only left tuffet, but dealt him a buffet
    Which doubled him up in a sailor knot.
It should be explained that at this he was pained:
    He cried: "I have vexed you, no doubt of it!
Your fist's like a truncheon." "You're still in my lunch-
        eon,"
    Was all that she answered. "Get out of it!"

And the *Moral* is this: Be it madam or miss
    To whom you have something to say,
You are only absurd when you get in the curd
    But you're rude when you get in the whey!

*Guy Wetmore Carryl*

# The Duel

The gingham dog and the calico cat
Side by side on the table sat;
'Twas half past twelve, and (what do you think!)
Nor one nor t'other had slept a wink!
    The old Dutch clock and the Chinese plate
    Appeared to know as sure as fate
There was going to be a terrible spat.
      *(I wasn't there: I simply state*
      *What was told to me by the Chinese plate!)*

The gingham dog went, "Bow-wow-wow!"
And the calico cat replied, "Mee-ow!"
The air was littered, an hour or so,
With bits of gingham and calico,
    While the old Dutch clock in the chimney-place
    Up with its hands before its face,
For it always dreaded a family row!
      *(Now mind; I'm only telling you*
      *What the old Dutch clock declares is true!)*

The Chinese plate looked very blue,
And wailed, "Oh, dear! what shall we do!"
But the gingham dog and the calico cat
Wallowed this way and tumbled that,

Employing every tooth and claw
In the awfullest way you ever saw—
And, oh! how the gingham and calico flew!
    (*Don't fancy I exaggerate—*
    *I got my news from the Chinese plate!*)


Next morning, where the two had sat
They found no trace of dog or cat:
And some folks think unto this day
That burglars stole that pair away!
    But the truth about the cat and pup
    Is this: they ate each other up!
Now what do you really think of that!
        (*The old Dutch clock it told me so,*
        *And that is how I came to know.*)

                    *Eugene Field*

# The Yarn of the "Nancy Bell"

'Twas on the shores that round our coast
   From Deal to Ramsgate span,
That I found alone, on a piece of stone,
   An elderly naval man.

His hair was weedy, his beard was long,
   And weedy and long was he;
And I heard this wight on the shore recite
   In a singular minor key:

"Oh, I am a cook and a captain bold,
   And the mate of the Nancy brig,
And a bo'sun tight, and a midshipmite,
   And the crew of the captain's gig."

And he shook his fists and he tore his hair,
   Till I really felt afraid,
For I couldn't help thinking the man had been drinking,
   And so I simply said:

"O elderly man, it's little I know
   Of the duties of men of the sea,
And I'll eat my hand if I understand
   How ever you can be

"At once a cook and a captain bold,
   And the mate of the Nancy brig,
And a bo'sun tight, and a midshipmite,
   And the crew of the captain's gig!"

Then he gave a hitch to his trowsers, which
   Is a trick all seamen larn,
And having got rid of a thumping quid,
   He spun this painful yarn:

" 'Twas in the good ship Nancy Bell
   That we sail'd to the Indian sea,
And there on a reef we come to grief,
   Which has often occurr'd to me.

"And pretty nigh all o' the crew was drown'd
   (There was seventy-seven o' soul):
And only ten of the Nancy's men
   Said 'Here!' to the muster-roll.

"There was me, and the cook, and the captain bold,
   And the mate of the Nancy brig,
And the bo'sun tight and a midshipmite,
   And the crew of the captain's gig.

"For a month we'd neither wittles nor drink,
   Till a-hungry we did fell,
So we draw'd a lot, and, accordin', shot
   The captain for our meal.

"The next lot fell to the Nancy's mate,
   And a delicate dish he made;
Then our appetite with the midshipmite
   We seven survivors stay'd.

"And then we murder'd the bo'sun tight,
   And he much resembled pig;
Then we wittled free, did the cook and me,
   On the crew of the captain's gig.

"Then only the cook and me was left,
   And the delicate question, 'Which
Of us two goes to the kettle?' arose,
   And we argued it out as sich.

"For I loved that cook as a brother, I did,
   And the cook he worshipp'd me;
But we'd both be blow'd if we'd either be stow'd
   In the other chap's hold, you see.

" 'I'll be eat if you dines off me,' says Tom.
   'Yes, that,' says I, 'you'll be.
I'm boil'd if I die, my friend,' quoth I;
   And 'Exactly so,' quoth he.

"Says he: 'Dear James, to murder me
   Were a foolish thing to do,
For don't you see that you can't cook *me*,
   While I can—and will—cook *you?*'

"So he boils the water, and takes the salt
  And the pepper in portions true
(Which he never forgot), and some chopp'd shallot,
  And some sage and parsley too.

" 'Come here,' says he, with a proper pride,
  Which his smiling features tell;
' 'Twill soothing be if I let you see
  How extremely nice you'll smell.'

"And he stirr'd round and round and round,
  And he sniff'd at the foaming froth;
When I ups with his heels, and smothers his squeals
  In the scum of the boiling broth.

"And I eat that cook in a week or less,
  And as I eating be
The last of his chops, why I almost drops,
  For a wessel in sight I see.

"And I never larf, and I never smile,
  And I never lark nor play;
But I sit and croak, and a single joke
  I have—which is to say:

"Oh, I am a cook and a captain bold,
  And the mate of the Nancy brig,
And a bo'sun tight, and a midshipmite,
  And the crew of the captain's gig!"

*W. S. Gilbert*

45

# The Fable of the Magnet and the Churn

A magnet hung in a hardware shop,
And all around was a loving crop
Of scissors and needles, nails and knives,
Offering love for all their lives;
But for iron the magnet felt no whim,
Though he charmed iron, it charmed not him;
From needles and nails and knives he'd turn,
For he'd set his love on a Silver Churn!

His most aesthetic,
Very magnetic
Fancy took this turn—
"If I can wheedle
A knife or a needle,
Why not a Silver Churn?"

And Iron and Steel expressed surprise,
The needles opened their well-drilled eyes,
The penknives felt "shut up," no doubt,
The scissors declared themselves "cut out,"
The kettles boiled with rage, 'tis said,
While every nail went off its head,

And hither and thither began to roam,
Till a hammer came up—and drove them home.

> While this magnetic,
> Peripatetic
> Lover he lived to learn,
> By no endeavor
> Can a magnet ever
> Attract a Silver Churn!

*W. S. Gilbert*

# The Grand Inquisitor's Song

I stole the prince and I brought him here
And left him, gaily prattling,
With a highly respectable gondolier,
Who promised the Royal babe to rear
And teach him the trade of a timoneer
With his own beloved brattling.
Both of the babes were strong and stout
And, considering all things, clever—
Of that there is no manner of doubt—
No probable possible shadow of doubt—
No possible doubt whatever.

Time sped, and when at the end of a year
I sought that infant cherished,
That highly respectable gondolier
Was lying a corpse on his humble bier—
I dropped a Grand Inquisitor's tear—
That gondolier had perished.
A taste for drink, combined with gout,
Had doubled him up forever.
Of that there is no manner of doubt,
No probable possible shadow of doubt,
No possible doubt whatever.

Now owing, I'm much disposed to fear,
To his terrible taste for tippling,
That highly respectable gondolier
Could never declare with a mind sincere
Which of the two was his offspring dear
And which the Royal stripling.
Which was which he could never make out,
Despite his best endeavor,
Of *that* there is no manner of doubt,
No probable possible shadow of doubt,
No possible doubt whatever.

The children followed his own career
(That statement can't be parried)
Of a highly respectable gondolier:
Well, one of the two who will soon be here—
But *which* of the two it is not quite clear—
Is the Royal Prince you married.
Search in and out and round about
And you'll discover never
A tale so free from every doubt,
All probable possible shadow of doubt,
All possible doubt whatever.

*W. S. Gilbert*

# The Elf and the Dormouse

Under a toadstool crept a wee Elf,
Out of the rain, to shelter himself.

Under the toadstool sound asleep,
Sat a big Dormouse all in a heap.

Trembled the wee Elf, frightened, and yet
Fearing to fly away lest he get wet.

To the next shelter—maybe a mile!
Sudden the wee Elf smiled a wee smile,

Tugged till the toadstool toppled in two.
Holding it over him, gayly he flew.

Soon he was safe home, dry as could be.
Soon woke the Dormouse—"Good gracious me.

"Where is my toadstool?" loud he lamented.
—And that's how umbrellas first were invented.

*Oliver Herford*

# The Dorchester Giant

There was a giant in times of old,
　A mighty one was he;
He had a wife, but she was a scold,
So he kept her shut in his mammoth fold;
　And he had children three.

It happened to be an election day,
　And the giants were choosing a king;
The people were not democrats then,
They did not talk of the rights of men,
　And all that sort of thing.

Then the giant took his children three,
　And fastened them in the pen;
The children roared; quoth the giant, "Be still!"
And Dorchester Heights and Milton Hill
　Rolled back the sound again.

Then he brought them a pudding stuffed with plums,
　As big as the State House dome;
Quoth he, "There's something for you to eat;
So stop your mouths with your 'lection treat,
　And wait till your dad comes home."

So the giant pulled him a chestnut stout,
    And whittled the boughs away;
The boys and their mother set up a shout,
Said he: "You're in, and you can't get out,
    Bellow as loud as you may."


Off he went, and he growled a tune
    As he strode the fields along;
'Tis said a buffalo fainted away,
And fell as cold as a lump of clay,
    When he heard the giant's song.


But whether the story's true or not,
    It isn't for me to show;
There's many a thing that's twice as queer
In somebody's lectures that we hear,
    And those are true you know.


What are those lone ones doing now,
    The wife and the children sad?
Oh, they are in a terrible rout,
Screaming, and throwing their pudding about,
    Acting as they were mad.


They flung it over to Roxbury hills,
    They flung it over the plain,
And all over Milton and Dorchester too
Great lumps of pudding the giants threw;
    They tumbled as thick as rain.

Giant and mammoth have passed away,
  For ages have floated by;
The suet is hard as a marrowbone,
And every plum is turned to a stone,
  But there the puddings lie.

And if, some pleasant afternoon,
  You'll ask me out to ride,
The whole of the story I will tell,
And you shall see where the puddings fell,
  And pay for the punch beside.

*Oliver Wendell Holmes*

# The Post That Fitted

Though tangled and twisted the course of true love,
   This ditty explains
No tangle's so tangled it cannot improve
   If the Lover has brains.

Ere the steamer bore him Eastward, Sleary was engaged
      to marry
An attractive girl at Tunbridge, whom he called "my
      little Carrie."
Sleary's pay was very modest; Sleary was the other way.
Who can cook a two-plate dinner on eight paltry dibs a
      day?

Long he pondered o'er the question in his scantly fur-
      nished quarters—
Then proposed to Minnie Boffkin, eldest of Judge Boff-
      kin's daughters.
Certainly an impecunious Subaltern was not a catch,
But the Boffkins knew that Minnie mightn't make an-
      other match.

So they recognized the business, and, to feed and clothe
      the bride,
Got him made a Something Something somewhere on the
      Bombay side,

54

Anyhow, the billet carried pay enough for him to marry—
As the artless Sleary put it: "Just the thing for me and
    Carrie."

Did he, therefore, jilt Miss Boffkin—impulse of a baser
    mind?
No! He started epileptic fits of an appalling kind.
(Of his *modus operandi* only this much I could gather:—
"Pears' shaving sticks will give you little taste and lots of
    lather.")

Frequently in public places his affliction used to smite
Sleary with distressing vigor—always in the Boffkins'
    sight.
Ere a week was over, Minnie weepingly returned his ring.
Told him his "unhappy weakness" stopped all thought of
    marrying.

Sleary bore the information with a chastened holy joy,—
Epileptic fits don't matter in Political employ,—
Wired three short words to Carrie—took his ticket,
    packed his kit—
Bade farewell to Minnie Boffkin in one last, long, linger-
    ing fit.

Four weeks later, Carrie Sleary read—and laughed until
    she wept—
Mrs. Boffkin's warning letter on the "wretched epilept."
Year by year, in pious patience, vengeful Mrs. Boffkin sits
Waiting for the Sleary babies to develop Sleary's fits.

*Rudyard Kipling*

# The Jumblies

They went to sea in a sieve, they did;
   In a sieve they went to sea;
In spite of all their friends could say,
On a winter's morn, on a stormy day,
   In a sieve they went to sea.
And when the sieve turned round and round,
And every one cried, "You'll all be drowned!"
They called aloud, "Our sieve ain't big;
But we don't care a button; we don't care a fig:
   In a sieve we'll go to sea!"
     Far and few, far and few,
      Are the lands where the Jumblies live:
      Their heads are green, and their hands are blue;
      And they went to sea in a sieve.

They sailed away in a sieve, they did,
   In a sieve they sailed so fast,
With only a beautiful pea-green veil
Tied with a ribbon, by way of a sail,
   To a small tobacco-pipe mast.
And every one said who saw them go,
"Oh! won't they be soon upset, you know?
For the sky is dark, and the voyage is long;
And, happen what may, it's extremely wrong
   In a sieve to sail so fast."

The water it soon came in, it did;
   The water it soon came in:
So, to keep them dry, they wrapped their feet
In a pinky paper all folded neat:
   And they fastened it down with a pin.
And they passed the night in a crockery-jar;
And each of them said, "How wise we are!
Though the sky be dark, and the voyage be long,
Yet we never can think we were rash or wrong,
   While round in our sieve we spin."

And all night long they sailed away;
   And, when the sun went down,
They whistled and warbled a moony song
To the echoing sound of a coppery gong,
   In the shade of the mountains brown,
"O Timballoo! How happy we are
When we live in a sieve and a crockery-jar!
And all night long, in the moonlight pale,
We sail away with a pea-green sail
   In the shade of the mountains brown."

They sailed to the Western Sea, they did,—
   To a land all covered with trees:
And they bought an owl, and a useful cart,
And a pound of rice, and a cranberry-tart,
   And a hive of silvery bees;
And they bought a pig, and some green jackdaws,
And a lovely monkey with lollipop paws,
And forty bottles of ring-bo-ree,
   **And** no end of Stilton cheese:

And in twenty years they all came back,—
   In twenty years or more;
And every one said, "How tall they've grown!
For they've been to the Lakes, and the Torrible Zone,
   And the hills of the Chankly Bore."
And they drank their health, and gave them a feast
Of dumplings made of beautiful yeast;
And every one said, "If we only live,
We, too, will go to sea in a sieve,
   To the hills of the Chankly Bore."
      Far and few, far and few,
         Are the lands where the Jumblies live:
         Their heads are green, and their hands are blue;
         And they went to sea in a sieve.

*Edward Lear*

# The Courtship of the Yonghy-Bonghy-Bò

On the Coast of Coromandel
  Where the early pumpkins blow,
    In the middle of the woods
  Lived the Yonghy-Bonghy-Bò.
Two old chairs, and half a candle,
One old jug without a handle,—
    These were all his worldly goods:
    In the middle of the woods,
    These were all the worldly goods,
  Of the Yonghy-Bonghy-Bò,
  Of the Yonghy-Bonghy-Bò.

Once, among the Bong-trees walking
  Where the early pumpkins blow,
    To a little heap of stones
  Came the Yonghy-Bonghy-Bò.
There he heard a Lady talking
To some milk-white Hens of Dorking,—
    " 'Tis the Lady Jingly Jones!
    On that little heap of stones
    Sits the Lady Jingly Jones!"
  Said the Yonghy-Bonghy-Bò.

"Lady Jingly! Lady Jingly!
  Sitting where the pumpkins blow,
    Will you come and be my wife?"
  Said the Yonghy-Bonghy-Bò.
"I am tired of living singly,—
On this coast so wild and shingly,—
    I'm a-weary of my life;
    If you'll come and be my wife,
    Quite serene would be my life!"
  Said the Yonghy-Bonghy-Bò.

"On this coast of Coromandel,
  Shrimps and water-cresses grow,
    Prawns are plentiful and cheap,"
  Said the Yonghy-Bonghy-Bò.
"You shall have my chairs and candle
And my jug without a handle!
    Gaze upon the rolling deep
    (Fish is plentiful and cheap);
    As the sea, my love is deep!"
  Said the Yonghy-Bonghy-Bò.

Lady Jingly answered sadly,
  And her tears began to flow,—
    "Your proposal comes too late,
  Mr. Yonghy-Bonghy-Bò!
I would be your wife most gladly!"
(Here she twirled her fingers madly,)
    "But in England I've a mate!
    Yes! you've asked me far too late,
    For in England I've a mate,
  Mr. Yonghy-Bonghy-Bò.

"Mr. Jones—(his name is Handel,—
    Handel Jones, Esquire, & Co.)
        Dorking fowls delights to send,
    Mr. Yonghy-Bonghy-Bò!
Keep, oh! keep your chairs and candle,
And your jug without a handle,—
        I can merely be your friend!
        —Should my Jones more Dorkings send,
        I will give you three, my friend!
    Mr. Yonghy-Bonghy-Bò.

"Though you've such a tiny body,
    And your head so large doth grow,—
        Though your hat may blow away,
    Mr. Yonghy-Bonghy-Bò!
Though you're such a Hoddy Doddy,—
Yet I wish that I could modi-
        fy the words I needs must say!
        Will you please to go away?
        That is all I have to say,
    Mr. Yonghy-Bonghy-Bò!"

Down the slippery slopes of Myrtle,
    Where the early pumpkins blow,
        To the calm and silent sea
    Fled the Yonghy-Bonghy-Bò.
There, beyond the bay of Gurtle,
Lay a large and lively Turtle;—
        "You're the Cove," he said, "for me;
        On your back beyond the sea,
        Turtle, you shall carry me!"
    Said the Yonghy-Bonghy-Bò.

Through the silent-roaring ocean
   Did the Turtle swiftly go;
      Holding fast upon his shell
   Rode the Yonghy-Bonghy-Bò.
With a sad primeval motion
Towards the sunset isles of Boshen
      Still the Turtle bore him well.
      Holding fast upon his shell,
        "Lady Jingly Jones, farewell!"
   Sang the Yonghy-Bonghy-Bò.

From the Coast of Coromandel
   Did that Lady never go;
      On that heap of stones she moans
   For the Yonghy-Bonghy-Bò.
On that Coast of Coromandel,
In his jug without a handle,
      Still she weeps and daily mourns;
      On that little heap of stones
        To her Dorking Hens she moans
   For the Yonghy-Bonghy-Bò,
   For the Yonghy-Bonghy-Bò.

*Edward Lear*

# Adventures of Isabel

Isabel met an enormous bear;
Isabel, Isabel, didn't care.
The bear was hungry, the bear was ravenous,
The bear's big mouth was cruel and cavernous.
The bear said, Isabel, glad to meet you,
How do, Isabel, now I'll eat you!
Isabel, Isabel, didn't worry,
Isabel didn't scream or scurry.
She washed her hands and she straightened her hair up,
Then Isabel quietly ate the bear up.

Once on a night as black as pitch
Isabel met a wicked old witch.
The witch's face was cross and wrinkled,
The witch's gums with teeth were sprinkled.
Ho, ho, Isabel! the old witch crowed,
I'll turn you into an ugly toad!
Isabel, Isabel, didn't worry,
Isabel didn't scream or scurry.
She showed no rage and she showed no rancor,
But she turned the witch into milk and drank her.

Isabel met a hideous giant,
Isabel continued self-reliant.

The giant was hairy, the giant was horrid,
He had one eye in the middle of his forehead.
Good morning, Isabel, the giant said,
I'll grind your bones to make my bread.
Isabel, Isabel, didn't worry,
Isabel didn't scream or scurry.
She nibbled the zwieback that she always fed off,
And when it was gone, she cut the giant's head off.

Isabel met a troublesome doctor,
He punched and he poked till he really shocked her.
The doctor's talk was of coughs and chills
And the doctor's satchel bulged with pills.
The doctor said unto Isabel,
Swallow this, it will make you well.
Isabel, Isabel, didn't worry,
Isabel didn't scream or scurry.
She took those pills from the pill-concocter,
And Isabel calmly cured the doctor.

*Ogden Nash*

# The Priest and the Mulberry-Tree

Did you hear of the curate who mounted his mare,
And merrily trotted along to the fair?
Of creature more tractable none ever heard,
At the height of her speed she would stop at a word;
But again with a word, when the curate said, *Hey!*
She put forth her mettle and galloped away.

As near to the gates of the city he rode,
While the sun of September all brilliantly glowed,
The good priest discovered, with eyes of desire,
A mulberry-tree in a hedge of wild briar;
On boughs long and lofty, in many a green shoot,
Hung large, black, and glossy, the beautiful fruit.

The curate was hungry and thirsty to boot;
He shrunk from the thorns, though he longed for the
        fruit;
With a word he arrested his courser's keen speed,
And he stood up erect on the back of his steed;
On the saddle he stood while the creature stood still,
And he gathered the fruit till he took his good fill.

"Sure never," he thought, "was a creature so rare,
So docile, so true, as my excellent mare;

Lo, here now I stand," and he gazed all around,
"As safe and as steady as if on the ground.
Yet how had it been, if some traveler this way,
Had, dreaming no mischief, but chanced to cry, *Hey!*"

He stood with his head in the mulberry-tree,
And he spoke out aloud in his fond reverie.
At the sound of the word the good mare made a push,
And down went the priest in the wild-briar bush!
He remembered too late, on his thorny green bed,
Much that well may be thought cannot wisely be said.

*Thomas Love Peacock*

# Pyramus and Thisbe

This tragical tale, which, they say, is a true one,
Is old; but the manner is wholly a new one.
One Ovid, a writer of some reputation,
Has told it before in a tedious narration;
In a style, to be sure, of remarkable fullness,
But which nobody reads on account of its dullness.

Young Peter Pyramus,—*I* call him Peter,
Not for the sake of the rhyme or the meter,
But merely to make the name completer,—
For Peter lived in the olden times,
And in one of the worst of pagan climes
That flourish now in classical fame,
Long before either noble or boor
Had such a thing as a *Christian* name,—
Young Peter, then, was a nice young beau
As any young lady would wish to know;
In years, I ween, he was rather green,
That is to say, he was just eighteen,—
A trifle too short, and a shaving too lean,
But "a nice young man" as ever was seen,
And fit to dance with a May-day queen!

Now Peter loved a beautiful girl
As ever ensnared the heart of an earl
In the magical trap of an auburn curl,—

A little Miss Thisbe, who lived next door
(They slept, in fact, on the very same floor,
With a wall between them, and nothing more,—
Those double dwellings were common of yore),
And they loved each other, the legends say,
In that very beautiful, bountiful way,
That every young maid and every young blade
Are wont to do before they grow staid,
And learn to love by the laws of the trade.
But (alack-a-day, for the girl and the boy!)
A little impediment checked their joy,
And gave them, awhile, the deepest annoy.—
For some good reason, which history cloaks,
The match didn't happen to please the old folks!


So Thisbe's father and Peter's mother
Began the young couple to worry and bother,
And tried their innocent passion to smother
By keeping the lovers from seeing each other!
But who ever heard of a marriage deterred
Or even deferred
By any contrivance so very absurd
As scolding the boy, and caging his bird?


Now, Peter, who wasn't discouraged at all
By obstacles such as the timid appal,
Contrived to discover a hole in the wall,
Which wasn't so thick but removing a brick
Made a passage,—though rather provokingly small.

Through this little chink the lover could greet her,
And secrecy made their courting the sweeter,
While Peter kissed Thisbe, and Thisbe kissed Peter,
For kisses, like folks with diminutive souls,
Will manage to creep through the smallest of holes!


'Twas here that the lovers, intent upon love,
Laid a nice little plot to meet at a spot
Near a mulberry-tree in a neighboring grove;
For the plan was all laid by the youth and the maid,
Whose hearts, it would seem, were uncommonly bold
    ones,
To run off and get married in spite of the old ones.


In the shadows of evening, as still as a mouse,
The beautiful maiden slipped out of the house,
The mulberry-tree impatient to find;
While Peter, the vigilant matrons to blind,
Strolled leisurely out some minutes behind.


While waiting alone by the trysting-tree,
A terrible lion as e'er you set eye on
Came roaring along quite horrid to see,
And caused the young maiden in terror to flee;
(A lion's a creature whose regular trade is
Blood,—and "a terrible thing among ladies,")
And, losing her veil as she ran from the wood,
The monster bedabbled it over with blood.

Now, Peter, arriving, and seeing the veil
All covered o'er and reeking with gore,
Turned, all of a sudden, exceedingly pale,
And sat himself down to weep and to wail;
For, soon as he saw the garment, poor Peter
Made up his mind in very short meter
That Thisbe was dead, and the lion had eat her!
So breathing a prayer, he determined to share
The fate of his darling, "the loved and the lost,"
And fell on his dagger, and gave up the ghost!

Now Thisbe returning, and viewing her beau
Lying dead by her veil (which she happened to know),
She guessed in a moment, the cause of his erring,
And, seizing the knife, that had taken his life,
In less than a jiffy was dead as a herring!

### MORAL

Young gentlemen: Pray recollect, if you please,
Not to make assignations near mulberry-trees;
Should your mistress be missing, it shows a weak head
To be stabbing yourself, till you know she is dead.

Young ladies: You shouldn't go strolling about
When your anxious mammas don't know you are out;
And remember that accidents often befall
From kissing young fellows through holes in the wall.

*John Godfrey Saxe*

# Meddlesome Matty

One ugly trick has often spoiled
   The sweetest and the best;
Matilda, though a pleasant child,
   One ugly trick possessed,
Which, like a cloud before the skies,
Hid all her better qualities.

Sometimes she'd lift the tea-pot lid,
   To peep at what was in it;
Or tilt the kettle, if you did
   But turn your back a minute.
In vain you told her not to touch,
Her trick of meddling grew so much.

Her grandmamma went out one day,
   And by mistake she laid
Her spectacles and snuff-box gay
   Too near the little maid;
"Ah! well," thought she, "I'll try them on,
As soon as grandmamma is gone."

Forthwith she placed upon her nose
   The glasses large and wide;

And looking round, as I suppose,
　　The snuff-box too she spied:
"Oh! what a pretty box is that;
I'll open it," said little Matt.

"I know that grandmamma would say,
　　'Don't meddle with it, dear';
But then she's far enough away,
　　And no one else is near:
Besides what can there be amiss
In opening such a box as this?"

So thumb and finger went to work
　　To move the stubborn lid,
And presently a mighty jerk
　　The mighty mischief did;
For all at once, ah! woeful case,
The snuff came puffing in her face.

Poor eyes, and nose, and mouth, beside,
　　A dismal sight presented;
In vain, as bitterly she cried,
　　Her folly she repented.
In vain she ran about for ease;
She could do nothing now but sneeze.

She dashed the spectacles away,
　　To wipe her tingling eyes.
And as in twenty bits they lay,
　　Her grandmamma she spies.
"Heyday! and what's the matter now?"
Cried grandmamma, with lifted brow.

Matilda, smarting with the pain,
And tingling still, and sore,
Made many a promise to refrain
From meddling evermore.
And 'tis a fact, as I have heard,
She ever since has kept her word.

*Ann Taylor*

# A Tragic Story

There lived a sage in days of yore,
And he a handsome pigtail wore;
But wondered much, and sorrowed more,
　　Because it hung behind him.

He mused upon this curious case,
And swore he'd change the pigtail's place,
And have it hanging at his face,
　　Not dangling there behind him.

Says he, "The mystery I've found,—
I'll turn me round,"—he turned him round;
　　But still it hung behind him.

Then round and round, and out and in,
All day the puzzled sage did spin;
In vain—it mattered not a pin,—
　　The pigtail hung behind him.

And right, and left, and round about,
And up, and down, and in, and out
He turned; but still the pigtail stout
　　Hung steadily behind him.

And though his efforts never slack,
And though he twist, and twirl, and tack,
Alas! still faithful to his back,
    The pigtail hangs behind him.

*William Makepeace Thackeray*

# Casey's Revenge

BEING A REPLY TO THE FAMOUS BASEBALL CLASSIC,
"CASEY AT THE BAT"

There were saddened hearts in Mudville for a week or
    even more;
There were muttered oaths and curses—every fan in town
    was sore.
"Just think," said one, "how soft it looked with Casey at
    the bat!
And then to think he'd go and spring a bush-league trick
    like that."


All his past fame was forgotten; he was now a hopeless
    "shine,"
They called him "Strike-out Casey" from the mayor down
    the line,
And as he came to bat each day his bosom heaved a sigh,
While a look of helpless fury shone in mighty Casey's eye.


The lane is long, someone has said, that never turns
    again,
And Fate, though fickle, often gives another chance to
    men.

And Casey smiled—his rugged face no longer wore a
    frown;
The pitcher who had started all the trouble came to
    town.


All Mudville had assembled; ten thousand fans had come
To see the twirler who had put big Casey on the bum;
And when he stepped into the box the multitude went
    wild.
He doffed his cap in proud disdain—but Casey only
    smiled.


"Play ball!" the umpire's voice rang out, and then the
    game began;
But in that throng of thousands there was not a single fan
Who thought that Mudville had a chance; and with the
    setting sun
Their hopes sank low—the rival team was leading "four
    to one."


The last half of the ninth came round, with no change in
    the score;
But when the first man up hit safe the crowd began to
    roar.
The din increased, the echo of ten thousand shouts was
    heard
When the pitcher hit the second and gave "four balls" to
    the third.

Three men on base—nobody out—three runs to tie the
  game!
A triple meant the highest niche in Mudville's hall of
  fame;
But here the rally ended and the gloom was deep as night
When the fourth one "fouled to catcher" and the fifth
  "flew out to right."

A dismal groan in chorus came—a scowl was on each
  face—
When Casey walked up, bat in hand, and slowly took his
  place;
His bloodshot eyes in fury gleamed; his teeth were
  clinched in hate;
He gave his cap a vicious hook and pounded on the plate.

But fame is fleeting as the wind, and glory fades away;
There were no wild and woolly cheers, no glad acclaim
  this day.
They hissed and groaned and hooted as they clamored,
  "Strike him out!"
But Casey gave no outward sign that he had heard this
  shout.

The pitcher smiled and cut one loose; across the plate it
  spread;
Another hiss, another groan. "Strike one!" the umpire
  said.
Zip! Like a shot, the second curve broke just below his
  knee—
"Strike two!" the umpire roared aloud; but Casey made
  no plea.

No roasting for the umpire now—his was an easy lot;
But here the pitcher whirled again—was that a rifle shot?
A whack! a crack! and out through space the leather pel-
   let flew,
A blot against the distant sky, a speck against the blue.

Above the fence in center field, in rapid whirling flight,
The sphere sailed on; the blot grew dim and then was lost
   to sight.
Ten thousand hats were thrown in air, ten thousand
   threw a fit;
But no one ever found the ball that mighty Casey hit!

Oh, somewhere in this favored land dark clouds may hide
   the sun,
And somewhere bands no longer play and children have
   no fun;
And somewhere over blighted lives there hangs a heavy
   pall;
But Mudville hearts are happy now—for Casey hit the
   ball!

*James Wilson*

# How I Brought the Good News from Aix to Ghent (or Vice Versa)

(It) runs (or rather gallops) roughly as follows: we quote from memory (having no boots of reference at hand):

I sprang to the rollocks and Jorrocks and me,
And I galloped, you galloped, he galloped, we galloped
      all three . . .
Not a word to each other; we kept changing place,
Neck to neck, back to front, ear to ear, face to face;
And we yelled once or twice, when we heard a clock
      chime,
"Would you kindly oblige us, *Is that the right time?*"
As I galloped, you galloped, he galloped, we galloped, ye
      galloped, they two shall have galloped; *let us trot.*

\*    \*    \*    \*    \*

I unsaddled the saddle, unbuckled the bit,
Unshackled the bridle (the thing didn't fit)
And ungalloped, ungalloped, ungalloped, ungalloped a
      bit.
Then I cast off my bluff-coat, let my bowler hat fall,
Took off both my boots and my trousers and all—
Drank off my stirrup-cup, felt a bit tight,
And unbridled the saddle: it still wasn't right.

\* \* \* \* \*

Then all I remember is, things reeling round
As I sat with my head 'twixt my ears on the ground—
For imagine my shame when they asked what I meant
And I had to confess that I'd been, gone and went
And *forgotten the news* I was bringing to Ghent,
Though I'd galloped and galloped and galloped and gal-
     loped and galloped
And galloped and galloped and galloped. (Had I not
     would have been galloped?)


### ENVOI

So I sprang to a taxi and shouted "To Aix!"
And he blew on his horn and he threw off his brakes,
And all the way back till my money was spent
We rattled and rattled and rattled and rattled and rattled
And rattled and rattled—
And eventually sent a telegram.

*R. J. Yeatman and W. C. Sellar*

# Going Too Far

A woman who lived in Holland, of old,
Polished her brass till it shone like gold.
She washed her pig after all his meals
In spite of his energetic squeals.
She scrubbed her doorstep into the ground,
And the children's faces, pink and round,
She washed so hard that in several cases
She polished their features off their faces—
Which gave them an odd appearance, though
She thought they were really neater so!
Then her passion for cleaning quickly grew,
And she scrubbed and polished the village through,
Until, to the rage of all the people,
She cleaned the weather-vane off the steeple.
As she looked at the sky one summer's night
She thought that the stars shone out less bright;
And she said with a sigh, "If I were there,
I'd rub them up till the world should stare."
That night a storm began to brew,
And a wind from the ocean blew and blew
Till, when she came to her door next day
It whisked her up, and blew her away—
Up and up in the air so high
That she vanished, at last, in the stormy sky.

Since then it's said that each twinkling star
And the big white moon, shine brighter far.
But the neighbors shake their heads in fear
She may rub so hard they will disappear!

*Mildred Howells*

# Ballads | Old and New

# Robin Hood and the Widow's Three Sons

There are twelve months in all the year,
   As I hear many men say,
But the merriest month in all the year
   Is the merry month of May.

Now Robin Hood is to Nottingham gone,
   *With a link a down and a day,*
And there he met a silly old woman,
   Was weeping on the way.

"What news? what news, thou silly old woman?
   What news hast thou for me?"
Said she, "There's three squires in Nottingham town
   To-day is condemn'd to die."

"O have they parishes burnt?" he said,
   "Or have they ministers slain?
Or have they robb'd any virgin,
   Or other men's wives have ta'en?"

"They have no parishes burnt, good sir,
   Nor yet have ministers slain,
Nor have they robbed any virgin,
   Nor other men's wives have ta'en."

"O what have they done?" said bold Robin Hood,
 "I pray thee tell to me."
"It's for slaying of the King's fallow deer,
 Bearing their long bows with thee."


Now Robin Hood is to Nottingham gone,
 *With a link a down and a day,*
And there he met with a silly old palmer,
 Was walking along the highway.


"What news? what news, thou silly old man?
 What news, I do thee pray?"
Said he, "Three squires in Nottingham town
 Are condemned to die this day."


"Come change thy apparel with me, old man,
 Come change thy apparel for mine.
Here is forty shillings in good silver;
 Go drink it in beer or wine."


"O thine apparel is good," he said,
 "And mine is ragged and torn;
Wherever you go, wherever you ride,
 Laugh ne'er an old man to scorn."


"Come change thy apparel with me, old churl,
 Come change thy apparel with mine.
Here are twenty pieces of good broad gold;
 Go feast thy brethren with wine."

87

Then he put on the old man's cloak,
  Was patch'd black, blue, and red;
He thought no shame, all the day long,
  To wear the bags of bread.


Then he put on the old man's hose,
  Were patch'd from knee to wrist;
"By the truth of my body," said bold **Robin Hood**,
  "I'd laugh if I had any list." *


Then he put on the old man's shoes,
  Were patch'd both beneath and aboon;
Then Robin Hood swore a solemn oath,
  "It's good habit that makes a man!"


Now Robin Hood is to Nottingham gone,
  *With a link a down and a down,*
And there he met with the proud **Sheriff**,
  Was walking along the town.


"O save, O save, O Sheriff," he said,
  "O save, and you may see!
And what will you give to a silly old man
  To-day will your hangman be?"


"Some suits, some suits," the Sheriff he said,
  "Some suits I'll give to thee;
Some suits, some suits, and pence thirteen
  To-day's a hangman's fee."

* List: desire for it.

88

Then Robin he turns him round about,
  And jumps from stock to stone;
"By the truth of my body," the Sheriff he said,
  "That's well jumpt, thou nimble old man."


"I was ne'er a hangman in all my life,
  Nor yet intends to trade;
But curst be he," said bold Robin,
  "That first a hangman was made!"


"I've a bag for meal, and a bag for malt,
  And a bag for barley and corn;
A bag for bread, and a bag for beef,
  And a bag for my little small horn."


"I have a horn in my pocket,
  I got it from Robin Hood,
And still when I set it to my mouth,
  For thee it blows little good."


"O wind thy horn, thou proud fellow,
  Of thee I have no doubt;
I wish that thou give such a blast
  Till both thy eyes fall out."


The first loud blast that he did blow,
  He blew both loud and shrill;
A hundred and fifty of Robin Hood's men
  Came riding over the hill.

The next loud blast that he did give,
    He blew both loud and amain;
And quickly sixty of Robin Hood's men
    Came shining over the plain.

"O who are yon," the Sheriff said,
    "Come tripping over the lea?"
"They're my attendants," brave Robin did say,
    "They'll pay a visit to thee."

They took the gallows from the dale,
    They set it in the glen,
They hang'd the proud Sheriff on that,
    And releas'd their own three men.

*Traditional: English*

# The Wife of Usher's Well

There lived a wife at Usher's Well,
   And a wealthy wife was she;
She had three stout and stalwart sons,
   And sent them o'er the sea.

They hadna been a week from her
   A week but barely ane,
Whan word came to the carline wife,
   That her three sons were gane.

They hadna been a week from her,
   A week but barely three,
Whan word came to the carline wife,
   That her sons she'd never see.

"I wish the wind may never cease,
   Nor fashes in the flood,
Till my three sons come hame to me,
   In earthly flesh and blood!"

It fell about the Martinmas,
   When nights are lang and mirk,
The carline wife's three sons came hame,
   And their hats were o' the birk.

It neither grew in syke nor ditch,
  Nor yet in ony sheugh;
But at the gates o' Paradise,
  That birk grew fair eneugh.

"Blow up the fire, my maidens!
  Bring water from the well!
For a' my house shall feast this night,
  Since my three sons are well."

And she had made to them a bed,
  She's made it large and wide;
And she's ta'en her mantle her about,
  Sat down at the bed-side.

Up then crew the red, red cock,
  And up and crew the gray;
The eldest to the youngest said,
  " 'Tis time we were awa'."

The cock he hadna crawed but once,
  And clapped his wings at a',
Whan the youngest to the eldest said,
  "Brother, we must awa'.

"The cock doth craw, the day doth daw'.
  The channerin' worm doth chide;
Gin we be missed out o' our place,
  A sair pain we maun bide."

"Lie still, lie still, a little wee while,
  Lie still but if we may;

Gin my mother should miss us when she wakes,
  She'll go mad ere it be day."

O they've ta'en up their mother's mantle,
  And they've hinged it on the pin:
"O lang may ye hing, my mother's mantle,
  Ere ye hap us again!

"Fare-ye-weel, my mother dear!
  Fareweel to barn and byre!
And fare-ye-weel, the bonny lass
  That kindles my mother's fire."

                    *Traditional: English*

# Get Up and Bar the Door

It fell about the Martinmas time,
    And a gay time it was then,
When our goodwife got puddings to make,
    And she's boiled them in the pan.

The wind so cold blew south and north,
    And blew into the floor;
Quoth our goodman to our goodwife,
    "Get up and bar the door."

"My hand is in my household work,
    Goodman, as ye may see;
And it will not be barred for a hundred years,
    If it's to be barred by me!"

They made a pact between them both,
    They made it firm and sure,
That whoso'er should speak the first,
    Should rise and bar the door.

Then by there came two gentlemen,
    At twelve o'clock at night,
And they could see neither house nor hall,
    Nor coal nor candlelight.

"Now whether is this a rich man's house,
  Or whether is it a poor?"
But never a word would one of them speak,
  For barring of the door.

The guests they ate the white puddings,
  And then they ate the black;
Tho' much the goodwife thought to herself,
  Yet never a word she spake.

Then said one stranger to the other,
  "Here, man, take ye my knife;
Do ye take off the old man's beard,
  And I'll kiss the goodwife."

"There's no hot water to scrape it off,
  And what shall we do then?"
"Then why not use the pudding broth,
  That boils into the pan?"

O up then started our goodman,
  An angry man was he;
"Will ye kiss my wife before my eyes!
  And with pudding broth scald me!"

Then up and started our goodwife,
  Gave three skips on the floor:
"Goodman, you've spoken the foremost word.
  Get up and bar the door!"

*Traditional: English*

# The Execution of Montrose

(MAY 21, 1650)

Come hither, Evan Cameron!
  Come, stand beside my knee:
I hear the river roaring down
  Towards the wintry sea.
There's shouting on the mountain-side,
  There's war within the blast;
Old faces look upon me,
  Old forms go trooping past:
I hear the pibroch wailing
  Amidst the din of fight,
And my dim spirit wakes again
  Upon the verge of night.


'Twas I that led the Highland host
  Through wild Lochaber's snows,
What time the plaided clans came down
  To battle with Montrose.
I've told thee how the Southrons fell
  Beneath the broad claymore,
And how we smote the Campbell clan
  By Inverlochy's shore.

I've told thee how we swept Dundee,
   And tamed the Lindsay's pride;
But never have I told thee yet
   How the great Marquis died.


A traitor sold him to his foes;—
   O deed of deathless shame!
I charge thee, boy, if e'er thou meet
   With one of Assynt's name—
Be it upon the mountain's side,
   Or yet within the glen,
Stand he in martial gear alone,
   Or backed by armèd men—
Face him, as thou wouldst face the man
   Who wronged thy sire's renown;
Remember of what blood thou art,
   And strike the caitiff down!


They brought him to the Watergate,
   Hard bound with hempen span,
As though they held a lion there,
   And not a fenceless man.
They set him high upon a cart,—
   The hangman rode below,—
They drew his hands behind his back,
   And bared his noble brow.
Then, as a hound is slipped from leash,
   They cheered the common throng,
And blew the note with yell and shout,
   And bade him pass along.

It would have made a brave man's heart
  Grow sad and sick that day,
And every open window
  Was full as full might be
With black-robed Covenanting carles,
  That goodly sport to see!

But when he came, though pale and wan,
  He looked so great and high,
So noble was his manly front,
  So calm his steadfast eye,
The rabble rout forebore to shout,
  And each man held his breath,
For well they knew the hero's soul
  Was face to face with death.
And then a mournful shudder
  Through all the people crept,
And some that came to scoff at him
  Now turned aside and wept.

But onwards—always onwards,
  In silence and in gloom,
The dreary pageant labored,
  Till it reached the house of doom.
Then first a woman's voice was heard
  In jeer and laughter loud,
And an angry cry and a hiss arose
  From the heart of the tossing crowd:
Then, as the Graeme looked upwards,
  He saw the ugly smile
Of him who sold his king for gold,—
  The master-fiend Argyle!

The Marquis gazed a moment,
   And nothing did he say,
But Argyle's cheek grew ghastly pale
   And he turned his eyes away.
The painted harlot by his side,
   She shook through every limb,
For a roar like thunder swept the street,
   And hands were clenched at him:
And a Saxon soldier cried aloud,
   "Back, coward, from thy place!
For seven long years thou hast not dared
   To look him in the face."

Had I been there with sword in hand,
   And fifty Camerons by,
That day through high Dunedin's streets
   Had pealed the slogan-cry.
Not all their troops of trampling horse,
   Nor might of mailèd men,
Not all the rebels in the south
   Had borne us backwards then!
Once more his foot on Highland heath
   Had trod as free as air,
Or I, and all who bore my name,
   Been laid around him there!

It might not be. They placed him next
   Within the solemn hall,
Where once the Scottish kings were throned
   Amidst their nobles all.

But there was dust of vulgar feet
   On that polluted floor,
And perjured traitors filled the place
   Where good men sate before.
With savage glee came Warriston
   To read the murderous doom;
And then uprose the great Montrose
   In the middle of the room.


"Now, by my faith as belted knight,
   And by the name I bear,
And by the bright Saint Andrew's cross
   That waves above us there,
Yea, by a greater, mightier oath—
   And oh, that such should be!—
By that dark stream of royal blood
   That lies 'twixt you and me,—
I have not sought in battle-field
   A wreath of such renown,
Nor dared I hope on my dying day
   To win the martyr's crown!


"There is a chamber far away
   Where sleep the good and brave,
But a better place ye have named for me
   Than by my fathers' grave.
For truth and right, 'gainst treason's might,
   This hand hath always striven,
And ye raise it up for a witness still
   In the eye of earth and heaven.

Then nail my head on yonder tower,
  Give every town a limb,—
And God who made shall gather them:
  I go from you to Him!"


The morning dawned full darkly,
  The rain came flashing down,
And the jagged streak of the levin-bolt
  Lit up the gloomy town:
The thunder crashed across the heaven,
  The fatal hour was come;
Yet aye broke in, with muffled beat,
  The 'larum of the drum.
There was madness on the earth below
  And anger in the sky,
And young and old, and rich and poor,
  Came forth to see him die.


Ah, God! that ghastly gibbet!
  How dismal 'tis to see
The great tall spectral skeleton,
  The ladder and the tree!
Hark! hark! it is the clash of arms—
  The bells begin to toll—
"He is coming! he is coming!
  God's mercy on his soul!"
One last long peal of thunder:
  The clouds are cleared away,
And the glorious sun once more looks down
  Amidst the dazzling day.

"He is coming! he is coming!"
  Like a bridegroom from his room,
Came the hero from his prison
  To the scaffold and the doom.
There was glory on his forehead,
  There was luster in his eye,
And he never walked to battle
  More proudly than to die;
There was color in his visage,
  Though the cheeks of all were wan,
And they marvelled as they saw him pass,
  That great and goodly man!

He mounted up the scaffold,
  And he turned him to the crowd;
But they dared not trust the people,
  So he might not speak aloud.
But he looked upon the heavens,
  And they were clear and blue,
And in the liquid ether
  The eye of God shone through;
Yet a black and murky battlement
  Lay resting on the hill,
As though the thunder slept within—
  All else was calm and still.

The grim Geneva ministers
  With anxious scowl drew near,
As you have seen the ravens flock
  Around the dying deer.

He would not deign them word nor sign,
    But alone he bent the knee,
And veiled his face for Christ's dear grace
    Beneath the gallows-tree.
Then radiant and serene he rose,
    And cast his cloak away:
For he had ta'en his latest look
    Of earth and sun and day.

A beam of light fell o'er him
    Like a glory round the shriven,
And he climbed the lofty ladder
    As it were the path to heaven.
Then came a flash from out the cloud,
    And a stunning thunder-roll;
And no man dared to look aloft,
    For fear was on every soul.
There was another heavy sound,
    A hush and then a groan;
And darkness swept across the sky—
    The work of death was done!

*William Edmondstone Aytoun*

# The Abbot of Inisfalen

## I

The Abbot of Inisfalen
   Awoke ere dawn of day;
Under the dewy green leaves
   Went he forth to pray.

The lake around his island
   Lay smooth and dark and deep,
And, wrapped in a misty stillness,
   The mountains were all asleep.

Low kneeled the Abbot Cormac,
   When the dawn was dim and gray;
The prayers of his holy office
   He faithfully 'gan say.

Low kneeled the Abbot Cormac,
   When the dawn was waxing red,
And for his sins' forgiveness
   A solemn prayer he said.

Low kneeled that holy Abbot
   When the dawn was waxing clear;
And he prayed with loving-kindness
   For his convent brethren dear.

Low kneeled that blessed Abbot,
  When the dawn was waxing bright;
He prayed a great prayer for Ireland,
  He prayed with all his might.

Low kneeled that good old father,
  While the sun began to dart;
He prayed a prayer for all mankind,
  He prayed it from his heart.

II

The Abbot of Inisfalen
  Arose upon his feet;
He heard a small bird singing,
  And, oh, but it sung sweet!

He heard a white bird singing well
  Within a holly-tree;
A song so sweet and happy
  Never before heard he.

It sung upon a hazel,
  It sung upon a thorn;
He had never heard such music
  Since the hour that he was born.

It sung upon a sycamore,
  It sung upon a briar;
To follow the song and hearken
  This Abbot could never tire.

Till at last he well bethought him
   He might no longer stay;
So he blessed the little white singing-bird,
   And gladly went his way.


### III

But when he came to his Abbey walls,
   He found a wondrous change;
He saw no friendly faces there,
   For every face was strange.


The strangers spoke unto him;
   And he heard from all and each
The foreign tone of the Sassenach,
   Not wholesome Irish speech.


Then the oldest monk came forward,
   In Irish tongue spake he:
"Thou wearest the holy Augustine's dress,
   And who hath given it thee?"


"I wear the holy Augustine's dress,
   And Cormac is my name,
The Abbot of this good Abbey
   By grace of God I am.


"I went forth to pray, at the dawn of day;
   And when my prayers were said,
I hearkened awhile to a little bird
   That sung above my head."

The monks to him made answer,
    "Two hundred years have gone o'er,
Since our Abbot Cormac went through the gate,
    And never was heard of more.

"Matthias now is our Abbot,
    And twenty have passed away.
The stranger is lord of Ireland;
    We live in an evil day."

### IV

"Now give me absolution;
    For my time is come," said he.
And they gave him absolution
    As speedily as might be.

Then, close outside the window,
    The sweetest song they heard
That ever yet since the world began
    Was uttered by any bird.

The monks looked out and saw the bird,
    Its feathers all white and clean;
And there in a moment, beside it,
    Another white bird was seen.

Those two they sang together,
    Waved their white wings, and fled;
Flew aloft, and vanished;
    But the good old man was dead.

They buried his blessed body
  Where lake and greensward meet;
A carven cross above his head,
  A holly-bush at his feet;

Where spreads the beautiful water
  To gay or cloudy skies,
And the purple peaks of Killarney
  From ancient woods arise.

*William Allingham*

# A Ballad of Sir John Franklin

O, whither sail you, Sir John Franklin?
  Cried a whaler in Baffin's Bay.
To know if between the land and the pole
  I may find a broad sea-way.

I charge you back, Sir John Franklin,
  As you would live and thrive;
For between the land and the frozen pole
  No man may sail alive.

But lightly laughed the stout Sir John,
  And spoke unto his men:
Half England is wrong, if he be right;
  Bear off to westward then.

O, whither sail you, brave Englishman?
  Cried the little Esquimau.
Between your land and the polar star
  My goodly vessels go.

Come down, if you would journey there,
  The little Indian said;
And change your cloth for fur clothing,
  Your vessel for a sled.

But lightly laughed the stout Sir John,
  And the crew laughed with him too:—
A sailor to change from ship to sled,
  I ween, were something new.

All through the long, long polar day,
  The vessels westward sped;
And wherever the sail of Sir John was blown,
  The ice gave way and fled:—

Gave way with many a hollow groan,
  And with many a surly roar,
But it murmured and threatened on every side,
  And closed where he sailed before.

Ho! see ye not, my merry men,
  The broad and open sea?
Bethink ye what the whaler said,
Think of the little Indian's sled!
  The crew laughed in glee.

Sir John, Sir John, 'tis bitter cold,
  The scud drives on the breeze,
The ice comes looming from the north,
  The very sunbeams freeze.

Bright summer goes, dark winter comes,—
  We cannot rule the year;
But long ere summer's sun goes down,
  On yonder sea we'll steer.

The dripping icebergs dipped and rose,
    And floundered down the gale;
The ships were stayed, the yards were manned,
    And furled the useless sail.


The summer's gone, the winter's come,—
    We sail not on yonder sea:
Why sail we not, Sir John Franklin?—
    A silent man was he.


The summer goes, the winter comes—
    We cannot rule the year:
I ween we cannot rule the ways,
    Sir John, wherein we'd steer.


The cruel ice came floating on,
    And closed beneath the lee,
Till the thickening waters dashed no more:
'Twas ice around, behind, before—
    My God! there is no sea!


What think you of the whaler now?
    What of the Esquimau?
A sled were better than a ship,
    To cruise through ice and snow.


Down sank the baleful crimson sun,
    The northern light came out,
And glared upon the ice-bound ships,
    And shook its spears about.

The snow came down, storm breeding storm,
   And on the decks was laid,
Till the weary sailor, sick at heart,
   Sank down beside his spade.

Sir John, the night is black and long,
   The hissing wind is bleak,
The hard, green ice as strong as death:—
   I prithee, Captain, speak!

The night is neither bright nor short,
   The singing breeze is cold,—
The ice is not so strong as hope,
   The heart of man is bold!

What hope can scale this icy wall,
   High over the main flag-staff?
Above the ridges the wolf and bear
Look down, with a patient, settled stare,
   Look down on us and laugh.

The summer went, the winter came—
   We could not rule the year;
But summer will melt the ice again,
And open a path to the sunny main,
   Whereon our ships shall steer.

The winter went, the summer went,
   The winter came around;
But the hard, green ice was strong as death,
And the voice of hope sank to a breath,
   Yet caught at every sound.

Hark! heard you not the noise of guns?—
    And there, and there, again?
'Tis some uneasy iceberg's roar,
    As he turns in the frozen main.

Hurra! Hurra! the Esquimaux
    Across the ice-fields steal:
God give them grace for their charity!—
    Ye pray for the silly seal.

Sir John, where are the English fields,
    And where are the English trees,
And where are the little English flowers
    That open in the breeze?

Be still, be still, my brave sailors!
    You shall see the fields again,
And smell the scent of the opening flowers,
    The grass, and the waving grain.

Oh! when shall I see my orphan child?
    My Mary waits for me.
Oh! when shall I see my old mother,
    And pray at her trembling knee?

Be still, be still, my brave sailors!
    Think not such thoughts again.
But a tear froze slowly on his cheek:
    He thought of Lady Jane.

Ah! bitter, bitter grows the cold,
    The ice grows more and more;

More settled stare the wolf and bear
  More patient than before.

Oh, think you, good Sir John Franklin,
  We'll ever see the land?
'Twas cruel to send us here to starve,
  Without a helping hand.

'Twas cruel, Sir John, to send us here,
  So far from help or home,
To starve and freeze on this lonely sea:
I ween the lords of the Admiralty
  Would rather send than come.

Oh! whether we starve to death alone,
  Or sail to our own country,
We have done what man has never done—
The truth is founded, the secret won—
  We passed the Northern Sea!

*George Henry Baker*

# The Vision of Belshazzar

## (538 B.C.)

The King was on his throne,
　　The Satraps thronged the hall;
A thousand bright lamps shone
　　O'er that high festival.
A thousand cups of gold,
　　In Judah deemed divine,—
Jehovah's vessels hold
　　The godless Heathen's wine!

In that same hour and hall,
　　The fingers of a hand
Came forth against the wall,
　　And wrote as if on sand:
The fingers of a man;—
　　A solitary hand
Along the letters ran,
　　And traced them like a wand.

The monarch saw, and shook,
　　And bade no more rejoice;
All bloodless waxed his look,
　　And tremulous his voice.
"Let the men of lore appear,
　　The wisest of the earth,

And expound the words of fear,
  Which mar our royal mirth."


Chaldea's seers are good,
  But here they have no skill;
And the unknown letters stood,
  Untold and awful still.
And Babel's men of age
  Are wise and deep in lore;
But now they were not sage,
  They saw,—but knew no more.


A captive in the land,
  A stranger and a youth,
He heard the King's command,
  He saw that writing's truth.
The lamps around were bright,
  The prophecy in view:
He read it on that night,—
  The morrow proved it true.


"Belshazzar's grave is made,
  His kingdom passed away,
He, in the balance weighed,
  Is light and worthless clay;
The shroud, his robe of state,
  His canopy, the stone:
The Mede is at his gate!
  The Persian on his throne!"

*George Gordon Byron*

# The Three Fishers

Three fishers went sailing away to the West,
  Away to the West as the sun went down;
Each thought on the woman who loved him the best,
  And the children stood watching them out of the town;
For men must work, and women must weep,
And there's little to earn, and many to keep,
  Though the harbor bar be moaning.

Three wives sat up in the lighthouse tower
  And they trimmed the lamps as the sun went down;
They looked at the squall, and they looked at the shower,
  And the night-rack came rolling up ragged and brown.
But men must work, and women must weep,
Though storms be sudden, and waters deep,
  And the harbor bar be moaning.

Three corpses lay out on the shining sands
  In the morning gleam as the tide went down,
And the women are weeping and wringing their hands
  For those who will never come home to the town;
For men must work, and women must weep,
And the sooner it's over, the sooner to sleep;
  And good-by to the bar and its moaning.

*Charles Kingsley*

117

# The High Tide on the Coast of Lincolnshire

## (1571)

The old mayor climbed the belfry tower,
  The ringers ran by two, by three;
"Pull, if ye never pulled before;
  Good ringers, pull your best," quoth he.
"Play uppe, play uppe, O Boston bells!
Play all your changes, all your swells,
  Play uppe, 'The Brides of Enderby'."

Men say it was a stolen tyde—
  The Lord that sent it, He knows all;
But in myne ears doth still abide
  The message that the bells let fall:
And there was naught of strange, beside
The flight of mews and peewits pied
  By millions crouched on the old sea wall.

I sat and spun within the doore,
  My thread brake off, I raised myne eyes;
The level sun, like ruddy ore,
  Lay sinking in the barren skies;
And dark against day's golden death
She moved where Lindis wandereth,
My sonne's fair wife, Elizabeth.

"Cusha! Cusha! Cusha!" calling,
Ere the early dews were falling,
Farre away I heard her song,
"Cusha! Cusha!" all along;
Where the reedy Lindis floweth,
    Floweth, floweth,
From the meads where melick groweth
Faintly came her milking song—

"Cusha! Cusha! Cusha!" calling,
"For the dews will soone be falling;
Leave your meadow grasses mellow,
    Mellow, mellow;
Quit your cowslips, cowslips yellow;
Come uppe, Whitefoot, come uppe, Lightfoot;
Quit the stalks of parsley hollow,
    Hollow, hollow;
Come uppe, Jetty, rise and follow,
From the clovers lift your head;
Come uppe, Whitefoot, come uppe, Lightfoot,
Come uppe, Jetty, rise and follow,
Jetty, to the milking shed."

If it be long, ay, long ago,
    When I beginne to think howe long,
Againe I hear the Lindis flow,
    Swift as an arrowe, sharpe and strong;
And all the aire, it seemeth mee,
Bin full of floating bells (sayth shee),
That ring the tune of Enderby.

Alle fresh the level pasture lay,
  And not a shadowe mote be seene,
Save where full fyve good miles away
  The steeple towered from out the greene;
And lo! the great bell farre and wide
Was heard in all the country side
That Saturday at eventide.

The swanherds where their sedges are
  Moved on in sunset's golden breath,
The shepherde lads I heard afarre,
  And my sonne's wife, Elizabeth;
Till floating o'er the grassy sea
Came downe that kyndly message free,
The "Brides of Mavis Enderby."

Then some looked uppe into the sky,
  And all along where Lindis flows
To where the goodly vessels lie,
  And where the lordly steeple shows.
They sayde, "And why should this thing be?
What danger lowers by land or sea?
They ring the tune of Enderby!

"For evil news from Mablethorpe,
  Of pyrate galleys warping down;
For shippes ashore beyond the scorpe,
  They have not spared to wake the towne:
But while the west bin red to see,
And storms be none, and pyrates flee,
Why ring 'The Brides of Enderby'?"

I looked without, and lo! my sonne
 Came riding downe with might and main:
He raised a shout as he drew on,
 Till all the welkin rang again,
"Elizabeth! Elizabeth!"
(A sweeter woman ne'er drew breath
Than my sonne's wife, Elizabeth.)

"The olde sea wall (he cried) is downe,
 The rising tide comes on apace,
And boats adrift in yonder towne
 Go sailing uppe the market-place."
He shook as one that looks on death:
"God save you, mother!" straight he saith;
"Where is my wife, Elizabeth?"

"Good sonne, where Lindis winds her way,
 With her two bairns I marked her long;
And ere yon bells beganne to play,
 Afar I heard her milking song."
He looked across the grassy lea,
To right, to left, "Ho, Enderby!"
They rang "The Brides of Enderby!"

With that he cried and beat his breast;
 For, lo! along the river's bed
A might eygre * reared his crest,
 And uppe the Lindis raging sped.
It swept with thunderous noises loud;
Shaped like a curling snow-white cloud,
Or like a demon in a shroud.

* A large tidal wave.

And rearing Lindis backward pressed,
   Shook all her trembling bankes amaine;
Then madly at the eygre's breast
   Flung uppe her weltering walls again.
Then bankes came downe with ruin and rout—
Then beaten foam flew round about—
Then all the mighty floods were out.

So farre, so fast the eygre drave,
   The heart had hardly time to beat
Before a shallow seething wave
   Sobbed in the grasses at oure feet:
The feet had hardly time to flee
Before it brake against the knee,
And all the world was in the sea.

Upon the roofe we sate that night,
   The noise of bells went sweeping by;
I marked the lofty beacon light
   Stream from the church tower, red and high—
A lurid mark and dread to see;
And awsome bells they were to mee,
That in the dark rang "Enderby."

They rang the sailor lads to guide
   From roofe to roofe who fearless rowed;
And I—my sonne was at my side,
   And yet the ruddy beacon glowed:
And yet he moaned beneath his breath,
"O come in life, or come in death!
O lost! my love, Elizabeth!"

And didst thou visit him no more?
  'Thou didst, thou didst, my daughter deare;
The waters laid thee at his doore,
  Ere yet the early dawn was clear.
Thy pretty bairns in fast embrace,
The lifted sun shone on thy face,
Downe drifted to thy dwelling-place.

That flow strewed wrecks about the grass,
  That ebbe swept out the flocks to sea;
A fatal ebbe and flow, alas!
  To manye more than myne and mee;
But each will mourn his own (she saith);
And sweeter woman ne'er drew breath
Than my sonne's wife, Elizabeth.

I shall never hear her more
By the reedy Lindis shore,
"Cusha! Cusha! Cusha!" calling,
Ere the early dews be falling;
I shall never hear her song,
"Cusha! Cusha!" all along
Where the sunny Lindis floweth,
    Goeth, floweth;
From the meads where melick groweth,
  When the water winding down,
  Onward floweth to the town.

I shall never see her more
Where the reeds and rushes quiver,
    Shiver, quiver;
Stand beside the sobbing river,

Sobbing. throbbing, in its falling
To the sandy lonesome shore;
I shall never hear her calling,
"Leave your meadow grasses mellow,
     Mellow, mellow;
Quit your cowslips, cowslips yellow;
Come uppe, Whitefoot, come uppe, Lightfoot;
Quit your pipes of parsley hollow,
     Hollow, hollow;
Come uppe, Lightfoot, rise and follow;
     Lightfoot, Whitefoot,
From your clovers lift the head;
Come uppe, Jetty, follow, follow,
Jetty, to the milking shed."

*Jean Ingelow*

# God's Judgment on a Wicked Bishop

The summer and autumn had been so wet,
That in winter the corn was growing yet:
'Twas a piteous sight to see, all around,
The grain lie rotting on the ground.

Every day the starving poor
Crowded around Bishop Hatto's door;
For he had a plentiful last-year's store,
And all the neighborhood could tell
His granaries were furnished well.

At last Bishop Hatto appointed a day
To quiet the poor without delay;
He bade them to his great barn repair,
And they should have food for the winter there.

Rejoiced such tidings good to hear,
The poor folk flocked from far and near;
The great barn was full as it could hold
Of women and children, and young and old.

Then, when he saw it could hold no more,
Bishop Hatto made fast the door;

And, while for mercy on Christ they call,
He set fire to the barn, and burnt them all.

"I' faith, 'tis an excellent bonfire!" quoth he;
"And the country is greatly obliged to me
For ridding it, in these times forlorn,
Of rats that only consume the corn."

So then to his palace returned he,
And he sat down to supper merrily,
And he slept that night like an innocent man;
But Bishop Hatto never slept again.

In the morning, as he entered the hall,
Where his picture hung against the wall,
A sweat like death all over him came,
For the rats had eaten it out of the frame.

As he looked, there came a man from his farm,—
He had a countenance white with alarm:
"My Lord, I opened your granaries this morn,
And the rats had eaten all your corn."

Another came running presently,
And he was pale as pale could be.
"Fly! my Lord Bishop, fly!" quoth he,
"Ten thousand rats are coming this way,—
The Lord forgive you for yesterday!"

"I'll go to my tower in the Rhine," replied he;
" 'Tis the safest place in Germany,—

The walls are high, and the shores are steep,
And the tide is strong, and the water deep."

Bishop Hatto fearfully hastened away,
And he crossed the Rhine without delay,
And reached his tower, and barred with care
All the windows, and doors, and loop-holes there.

He laid him down and closed his eyes,
But soon a scream made him arise;
He started, and saw two eyes of flame
On his pillow, from whence the screaming came.

He listened and looked,—it was only the cat;
But the Bishop he grew more fearful for that,
For she sat screaming, mad with fear,
At the army of rats that were drawing near.

For they have swum over the river so deep,
And they have climbed the shores so steep,
And now by thousands up they crawl
To the holes and the windows in the wall.

Down on his knees the Bishop fell,
And faster and faster his beads did he tell,
As louder and louder, drawing near,
The saw of their teeth without he could hear.

And in at the windows, and in at the door,
And through the walls by thousands they pour;

And down from the ceiling and up through the floor,
From the right and the left, from behind and before,
From within and without, from above and below,—
And all at once to the Bishop they go.

They have whetted their teeth against the stones,
And now they pick the Bishop's bones;
They gnawed the flesh from every limb,
For they were sent to do judgment on him!

*Robert Southey*

# Pocahontas

Wearied arm and broken sword
  Wage in vain the desperate fight;
Round him press a countless horde,
  He is but a single knight.
Hark! a cry of triumph shrill
  Through the wilderness resounds,
  As, with twenty bleeding wounds,
Sinks the warrior, fighting still.

Now they heap the funeral pyre,
  And the torch of death they light;
Ah! 't is hard to die by fire!
  Who will shield the captive knight?
Round the stake with fiendish cry
  Wheel and dance the savage crown,
  Cold the victim's mien and proud,
And his breast is bared to die.

Who will shield the fearless heart?
  Who avert the murderous blade?
From the throng with sudden start
  See, there springs an Indian maid.

Quick she stands before the knight:
"Loose the chain, unbind the ring!
I am daughter of the king,
And I claim the Indian right!"

Dauntlessly aside she flings
Lifted axe and thirsty knife,
Fondly to his heart she clings,
And her bosom guards his life!
In the woods of Powhatan,
Still 't is told by Indian fires
How a daughter of their sires
Saved a captive Englishman.

*William Makepeace Thackeray*

# The River of Stars

## (A TALE OF NIAGARA)

*The lights of a hundred cities are fed by its midnight*
*    power.*
*Their wheels are moved by its thunder. But they, too,*
*    have their hour.*
*The tale of the Indian lovers, a cry from the years that are*
*    flown,*
*        While the river of stars is rolling,*
*        Rolling away to the darkness,*
*Abides with the power in the midnight, where love may*
*    find its own.*


She watched from the Huron tents till the first star shook
    in the air.
The sweet pine scented her fawn-skins, and breathed
    from her braided hair.
Her crown was of milk-white blood-root, because of the
    tryst she would keep,
        Beyond the river of beauty
        That drifted away in the darkness
Drawing the sunset thro' lilies, with eyes like stars, to the
    deep.

He watched, like a tall young wood-god, from the red
    pine that she named;
But not for the peril behind him, where the eyes of the
    Mohawks flamed.
Eagle-plumed he stood. But his heart was hunting afar,
    Where the river of longing whispered . . .
      And one swift shaft from the darkness
Felled him, her name in his death-cry, his eyes on the sun-
    set star.

\*    \*    \*    \*    \*

She stole from the river and listened. The moon on her
    wet skin shone.
As a silver birch in a pine-wood, her beauty flashed and
    was gone.
There was no wave in the forest. The dark arms closed
    her round.
    But the river of life went flowing,
      Flowing away to the darkness,
For her breast grew red with his heart's blood, in a night
    where the stars are drowned.

*Teach me, O my lover, as you taught me of love in a day,*
*Teach me of death, and for ever, and set my feet on the*
    *way,*
*To the land of the happy shadows, the land where you are*
    *flown.*
    —And the river of death went weeping,
      Weeping away to the darkness.—
*Is the hunting good, my lover, so good that you hunt*
    *alone?*

She rose to her feet like a shadow. She sent a cry thro' the
    night,
*Sa-sa-kuon,* the death-whoop, that tells of triumph in
    fight.
It broke from the bell of her mouth like the cry of a
    wounded bird,
    But the river of agony swelled it
      And swept it along to the darkness,
And the Mohawks, crouched in the darkness, leapt to
    their feet as they heard.


Close as the ring of the clouds that menace the moon with
    death,
At once they circled her round. Her bright breast panted
    for breath.
With only her own wild glory keeping the wolves at bay,
    While the river of parting whispered,
      Whispered away to the darkness,
She looked in their eyes for a moment, and strove for a
    word to say.


*Teach me, O my lover!*—She set her foot on the dead.
She laughed on the painted faces with their rings of
    yellow and red,—
*I thank you, wolves of the Mohawk, for a woman's hands
    might fail.*—
    —And the river of vengeance chuckled,
      Chuckled away to the darkness,—
*But ye have killed where I hunted. I have come to the
    end of my trail.*

*I thank you, braves of the Mohawk, who laid this thief at
    my feet.*
*He tore my heart out living, and tossed it his dogs to eat.*
*Ye have taught him of death in a moment, as he taught
    me of love in a day.*
    —And the river of passion deepened,
    Deepened and rushed to the darkness.—
*And yet may a woman requite you, and set your feet on
    the way.*

*For the woman that spits in my face, and the shaven heads
    that gibe,*
*This night shall a woman show you the tents of the
    Huron tribe.*
*They are lodged in a deep valley. With all things good it
    abounds.*
    *Where the red-eyed, green-mooned river*
    *Glides like a snake to the darkness,*
*I will show you a valley, Mohawks, like the Happy Hunt-
    ing Grounds.*

*Follow!* They chuckled, and followed like wolves to the
    glittering stream.
Shadows obeying a shadow, they launched their canoes in
    a dream.
Alone, in the first, with the blood on her breast, and her
    milk-white crown,
    She stood. She smiled at them, *Follow,*
    Then urged her canoe to the darkness,
And, silently flashing their paddles, the Mohawks fol-
    lowed her down.

\*　　\*　　\*　　\*　　\*

And now—as they slid thro' the pine-woods with their
    peaks of midnight blue,
She heard, in the broadening distance, the deep sound
    that she knew,
A mutter of steady thunder that grew as they glanced
    along;
    But ever she glanced before them
      And danced away to the darkness,
And or ever they heard it rightly, she raised her voice in
    a song:—


*The wind from the Isles of the Blesséd, it blows across the
    foam.*
*It sings in the flowing maples of the land that was my
    home.*
*Where the moose is a morning's hunt, and the buffalo
    feeds from the hand.—*
    And the river of mockery broadened,
    Broadened and rolled to the darkness—
*And the green maize lifts its feathers, and laughs the snow
    from the land.*


The river broadened and quickened. There was nought
    but river and sky.
The shores were lost in the darkness. She laughed and
    lifted a cry:

135

*Follow me! Sa-sa-kuon!* Swifter and swifter they swirled—
  And the flood of their doom went flying,
    Flying away to the darkness,
*Follow me, follow me, Mohawks, ye are shooting the edge*
  *of the world.*


They struggled like snakes to return. Like straws they
  were whirled on her track.
For the whole flood swooped to that edge where the unplumbed night dropt black,
The whole flood dropt to a thunder in an unplumbed
  hell beneath,
    And over the gulf of the thunder
    A mountain of spray from the darkness
Rose and stood in the heavens, like a shrouded image of
  death.


She rushed like a star before them. The moon on her
  glorying shone.
*Teach me, O my lover,*—her cry flashed out and was gone.
A moment they battled behind her. They lashed with
  their paddles and lunged;
    Then the Mohawks, turning their faces
    Like a blood-stained cloud to the darkness,
Over the edge of Niagara swept together and plunged.


*And the lights of a hundred cities are fed by the ancient*
  *power;*
*But a cry returns with the midnight; for they, too, have*
  *their hour.*

*Teach me, O my lover, as you taught me of love in a day.*
    *—While the river of stars is rolling,*
        *Rolling away to the darkness,—*
*Teach me of death, and for ever, and set my feet on the*
    *way!*

Alfred Noyes

# A Ballad of a Nun

From Eastertide to Eastertide
   For ten long years her patient knees
Engraved the stones—the fittest bride
   Of Christ in all the diocese.

She conquered every earthly lust;
   The abbess loved her more and more;
And, as a mark of perfect trust,
   Made her keeper of the door.

High on a hill the convent hung,
   Across a duchy looking down,
Where everlasting mountains flung
   Their shadows over tower and town.

The jewels of their lofty snows
   In constellations flashed at night;
Above their crests the moon arose;
   The deep earth shuddered with delight.

Long ere she left her cloudy bed,
   Still dreaming in the orient land,
On many a mountain's happy head
   Dawn lightly laid her rosy hand.

The adventurous sun took Heaven by storm;
  Clouds scattered largesses of rain;
The sounding cities, rich and warm,
  Smouldered and glittered in the plain.


Sometimes it was a wandering wind,
  Sometimes the fragrance of the pine,
Sometimes the thought how others sinned,
  That turned her sweet blood into wine.


Sometimes she heard a serenade
  Complaining sweetly far away:
She said, "A young man woos a maid";
  And dreamt of love till break of day.


Then would she ply her knotted scourge
  Until she swooned; but evermore
She had the same red sin to purge,
  Poor, passionate keeper of the door!


For still night's starry scroll unfurled,
  And still the day came like a flood:
It was the greatness of the world
  That made her long to use her blood.


In winter-time when Lent drew nigh,
  And hill and plain were wrapped in snow,
She watched beneath the frosty sky
  The nearest city nightly glow.

Like peals of airy bells outworn
  Faint laughter died above her head
In gusts of broken music borne:
  "They keep the Carnival," she said.


Her hungry heart devoured the town:
  "Heaven save me by a miracle!
Unless God sends an angel down,
  Thither I go though it were Hell."


She dug her nails deep in her breast,
  Sobbed, shrieked, and straight withdrew the bar:
A fledgling flying from the nest,
  A pale moth rushing to a star.


Fillet and veil in strips she tore;
  Her golden tresses floated wide;
The ring and bracelet that she wore
  As Christ's betrothed, she cast aside.


"Life's dearest meaning I shall probe;
  Lo! I shall taste of love at last!
Away!" She doffed her outer robe,
  And sent it sailing down the blast.


Her body seemed to warm the wind;
  With bleeding feet o'er ice she ran:
"I leave the righteous God behind;
  I go to worship sinful man."

She reached the sounding city's gate;
　　No question did the warder ask:
He passed her in: "Welcome, wild mate!"
　　He thought her some fantastic mask.

Half-naked through the town she went;
　　Each footstep left a bloody mark;
Crowds followed her with looks intent;
　　Her bright eyes made the torches dark.

Alone and watching in the street
　　There stood a grave youth nobly dressed;
To him she knelt and kissed his feet;
　　Her face her great desire confessed.

He healed her bosom with a kiss;
　　She gave him all her passion's hoard;
And sobbed and murmured ever, "This
　　Is life's great meaning, dear, my lord.

"I care not for my broken vow;
　　Though God should come in thunder soon,
I am sister to the mountains now,
　　And sister to the sun and moon."

Through all the towns of Belmarie
　　She made a progress like a queen.
"She is," they said, "what'er she be,
　　The strangest woman ever seen.

"From fairyland she must have come,
  Or else she is a mermaiden."
Some said she was a ghoul, and some
  A heathen goddess born again.

But soon her fire to ashes burned;
  Her beauty changed to haggardness;
Her golden hair to silver turned;
  The hour came of her last caress.

At midnight from her lonely bed
  She rose, and said, "I have had my will."
The old ragged robe she donned, and fled
  Back to the convent on the hill.

Half-naked as she went before,
  She hurried to the city wall,
Unnoticed in the rush and roar
  And splendor of the carnival.

No question did the warder ask:
  Her ragged robe, her shrunken limb,
Her dreadful eyes! "It is no mask;
  It is a she-wolf, gaunt and grim!"

She ran across the icy plain;
  Her worn blood curdled in the blast;
Each footstep left a crimson stain;
  The white-faced moon looked on aghast.

She said between her chattering jaws,
    "Deep peace is mine, I cease to strive;
Oh, comfortable convent laws,
    That bury foolish nuns alive!

"A trowel for my passing-bell,
    A little bed within the wall,
A coverlet of stones; how well
    I there shall keep the Carnival!"

Like tired bells chiming in their sleep,
    The wind faint peals of laughter bore;
She stopped her ears and climbed the steep,
    And thundered at the convent door.

It opened straight: she entered in,
    And at the wardress' feet fell prone:
"I come to purge away my sin:
    Bury me, close me up in stone."

The wardress raised her tenderly;
    She touched her wet and fast-shut eyes:
"Look, sister; sister, look at me;
    Look; can you see through my disguise?"

She looked and saw her own sad face,
    And trembled, wondering, "Who art thou?"
"God sent me down to fill your place:
    I am the Virgin Mary now."

And with the word, God's mother shone:
   The wanderer whispered, "Mary, hail!"
The vision helped her to put on
   Bracelet and fillet, ring and veil.

"You are sister to the mountains now,
   And sister to the day and night;
Sister to God." And on the brow
   She kissed her thrice, and left her sight.

While dreaming in her cloudy bed,
   Far in the crimson orient land,
On many a mountain's happy head
   Dawn lightly laid her rosy hand.

*John Davidson*

# Battles Long Ago

# The Destruction of Sennacherib

(710 B.C.)

The Assyrian came down like the wolf on the fold,
And his cohorts were gleaming in purple and gold;
And the sheen of their spears was like stars on the sea,
When the blue wave rolls nightly on deep Galilee.

Like the leaves of the forest when Summer is green,
That host with their banners at sunset were seen:
Like the leaves of the forest when Autumn hath blown,
That host on the morrow lay withered and strown.

For the Angel of Death spread his wings on the blast,
And breathed in the face of the foe as he passed;
And the eyes of the sleepers waxed deadly and chill,
And their hearts but once heaved, and for ever grew still!

And there lay the steed with his nostril all wide,
But through it there rolled not the breath of his pride:
And the foam of his gasping lay white on the turf,
And cold as the spray of the rock-beating surf.

And there lay the rider distorted and pale,
With the dew on his brow, and the rust on his mail;

And the tents were all silent, the banners alone,
The lances unlifted, the trumpet unblown.

And the widows of Ashur are loud in their wail,
And the idols are broke in the temple of Baal;
And the might of the Gentile, unsmote by the sword,
Hath melted like snow in the glance of the Lord!

*George Gordon Byron*

# The Battle of Otterburn

(AUGUST 10, 1388)

It fell about the Lammas tide,
   When muir-men win their hay,
That the doughty Earl of Douglas rade
   Into England, to take a prey.

He chose the Gordons and the Graemes,
   With them the Lindsays gay;
But the Jardines wald not with him ride,
   And they rue it to this day.

And they hae harried the dales o' Tyne,
   And half o' Bambrough-shire,
And the Otter-dale they burned it hale,
   And set it a' on fire.

Then he cam' up to Newcastle,
   And rade it round about:
"O wha's the lord of this castle?
   Or wha's the lady o't?"

But up spake proud Lord Percy then,
   And O but he spake hie!

"I am the lord of this castle,
  My wife's the lady gay."

"If thou'rt the lord of this castle,
  Sae weel it pleases me,
For, ere I cross the Border fells,
  The tane of us shall dee."

He took a lang spear in his hand,
  Shod with the metal free,
And for to meet the Douglas there
  He rode right furiouslie.

But O how pale his lady looked,
  Frae aff the castle-wa',
As down before the Scottish spear
  She saw proud Percy fa'.

"Had we twa been upon the green,
  And never an eye to see,
I wad hae had you, flesh and fell;
  But your sword shall gae wi me."

"Now gae ye up to Otterbourne,
  And wait there dayis three,
And gin I come not ere they end,
  A fause knight ca' ye me."

"The Otterbourne's a bonnie burn;
  'Tis pleasant there to be;
But there is naught at Otterbourne
  To feed my men and me.

"The deer rins wild on hill and dale,
  The birds fly wild frae tree to tree;
But there is neither bread nor kale
  To fend my men and me.

"Yet I will stay at Otterbourne,
  Where you sall welcome be;
And, if ye come not at three days' end,
  A fause lord I'll ca' thee."

"Thither will I come," proud Percy said.
  "By the might of Our Ladye";
"There will I bide thee," said the Douglas,
  "My troth I plight to thee."

They licted high on Otterbourne,
  Upon the bent sae broun;
They licted high on Otterbourne,
  And pitched their pallions doun.

And he that had a bonnie boy,
  He sent his horse to grass;
And he that had not a bonnie boy,
  His ain servant he was.

But up then spak' a little page,
  Before the peep o' dawn:
"O waken ye, waken ye, my good lord,
  For Percy's hard at hand."

"Ye lie, ye lie, ye liar loud!
  Sae loud I hear ye lie:

For Percy had not men yestreen
  To dight my men and me.

"But I hae dreamed a dreary dream,
  Beyond the Isle of Sky;
I saw a deid man win a fight,
  And I think that man was I."

He belted on his gude braid-sword,
  And to the field he ran,
But he forgot the hewmont strong,
  That should have kept his brain.

When Percy wi' the Douglas met,
  I wot he was fu' fain;
They swakkit swords, till sair they swat,
  And the blud ran down like rain.

But Percy wi' his gude braid-sword,
  That could sae sharply wound,
Has wounded Douglas on the brow,
  Till he fell to the ground.

And then he called his little foot-page,
  And said, "Run speedily,
And fetch my ain dear sister's son,
  Sir Hugh Montgomery."

"My nephew gude," the Douglas said,
  "What recks the death of ane?
Last night I dreamed a dreary dream,
  And I ken the day's thy ain!

"My wound is deep; I fain wad sleep;
   Tak' thou the vanguard o' the three,
And bury me by the braken-bush,
   That grows on yonder lilye lea.

"O bury me by the braken-bush,
   Beneath the blumin' brier;
Let never living mortal ken
   That a kindly Scot lies here."

He lifted up that noble lord,
   Wi' the saut tear in his e'e;
He hid him by the braken-bush,
   That his merrie men might not see.

The moon was clear, the day drew near,
   The spears in flinders flew,
And mony a gallant Englishman
   Ere day the Scotsmen slew.

The Gordons gude, in English blude
   They wat their hose and shoon;
The Lindsays flew like fire about,
   Till a' the fray was dune.

The Percy and Montgomery met,
   That either of other was fain;
They swakkit swords, and sair they swat,
   And the blude ran down between.

"Now yield thee, yield thee, Percy," he said,
   "Or else I will lay thee low!"

"To whom maun I yield," quoth Earl Percy,
  "Since I see it maun be so?"

"Thou shalt not yield to lord or loun,
  Nor yet shalt thou yield to me;
But yield thee to the braken-bush,
  That grows upon yon lilye lea."

"I will not yield to a braken-bush,
  Nor yet will I yield to a brier;
But I would yield to Earl Douglas,
  Or Sir Hugh Montgomery, if he were here."

As soon as he knew it was Montgomery,
  He struck his sword's point in the gronde;
The Montgomery was a courteous knight,
  And quickly took him by the honde.

This deed was done at the Otterbourne,
  About the breaking o' the day;
Earl Douglas was buried at the braken-bush,
  And the Percy led captive away.

*Traditional: Scots*

# The "Revenge"

## A BALLAD OF THE FLEET (SEPTEMBER, 1591)

At Florés in the Azores Sir Richard Grenville lay,
And a pinnace, like a fluttered bird, came flying from far
away:
"Spanish ships of war at sea! we have sighted fifty-three!"
Then sware Lord Thomas Howard: " 'Fore God I am no
coward;
But I cannot meet them here, for my ships are out of gear,
And the half my men are sick. I must fly, but follow
quick.
We are six ships of the line; can we fight with fifty-three?"

Then spake Sir Richard Grenville: "I know you are no
coward;
You fly them for a moment to fight with them again.
But I've ninety men and more that are lying sick ashore.
I should count myself the coward if I left them, my Lord
Howard,
To these Inquisition dogs and the devildoms of Spain."

So Lord Howard passed away with five ships of war that
day,
Till he melted like a cloud in the silent summer heaven;

But Sir Richard bore in hand all his sick men from the
    land
Very carefully and slow,
Men of Bideford in Devon,
And we laid them on the ballast down below;
For we brought them all aboard,
And they blessed him in their pain, that they were not
    left to Spain,
To the thumbscrew and the stake, for the glory of the
    Lord.

He had only a hundred seamen to work the ship and to
    fight,
And he sailed away from Florés till the Spaniard came in
    sight,
With his huge sea-castles heaving upon the weather bow.
"Shall we fight or shall we fly?
Good Sir Richard, tell us now,
For to fight is but to die!
There'll be little of us left by the time this sun be set."
And Sir Richard said again: "We be all good English
    men.
Let us bang these dogs of Seville, the children of the
    devil,
For I never turned my back upon Don or devil yet."

Sir Richard spoke and he laughed, and we roared a hur-
    rah, and so
The little *Revenge* ran on sheer into the heart of the foe,
With her hundred fighters on deck, and her ninety sick
    below;

For half of their fleet to the right and half to the left were
seen,

And the little *Revenge* ran on through the long sea-lane
between.

Thousands of their soldiers looked down from their decks
and laughed,

Thousands of their seamen made mock at the mad little
craft

Running on and on, till delayed

By their mountain-like *San Philip* that of fifteen hundred tons,

And up-shadowing high above us with her yawning tiers
of guns,

Took the breath from our sails, and we stayed.

And while now the great *San Philip* hung above us like a
cloud

Whence the thunderbolt will fall

Long and loud,

Four galleons drew away

From the Spanish fleet that day,

And two upon the larboard and two upon the starboard
lay,

And the battle-thunder broke from them all.

But anon the great *San Philip,* she bethought herself and
went,

And the rest they came aboard us, and they fought us
hand on hand,

For a dozen times they came with their pikes and mus-
    queteers,
And a dozen times we shook 'em off as a dog that shakes
    his ears
When he leaps from the water to the land.


And the sun went down, and the stars came out far over
    the summer sea,
But never a moment ceased the fight of the one and the
    fifty-three,
Ship after ship, the whole night long, their high-built
    galleons came,
Ship after ship, the whole night long, drew back with
    her dead and her shame.
For some were sunk and many were shattered, and so
    could fight us no more—
God of battles, was ever a battle like this in the world
    before?


For he said, "Fight on! fight on!"
Though his vessel was all but a wreck;
And it chanced that, when half of the short summer
    night was gone,
With a grisly wound to be dressed he had left the deck,
But a bullet struck him that was dressing it suddenly
    dead,
And himself he was wounded again in the side and the
    head,
And he said, "Fight on! fight on!"

And the night went down, and the sun smiled out far
over the summer sea,

And the Spanish fleet with broken sides lay round us all
in a ring;

But they dared not touch us again, for they feared that
we still could sting,

So they watched what the end would be.

And we had not fought them in vain,

But in perilous plight were we,

Seeing forty of our poor hundred were slain,

And half of the rest of us maimed for life

In the crash of the cannonades and the desperate strife;

And the sick men down in the hold were most of them
stark and cold,

And the pikes were all broken or bent, and the powder
was all of it spent;

And the masts and the rigging were lying over the side;

But Sir Richard cried in his English pride,

"We have fought such a fight for a day and a night

As may never be fought again!

We have won great glory, my men!

And a day less or more

At sea or ashore,

We die—does it matter when?

Sink me the ship, Master Gunner—sink her, split her in
twain!

Fall into the hands of God, not into the hands of Spain!"

And the gunner said, "Ay, ay," but the seamen made
reply:

"We have children, we have wives,

And the Lord hath spared our lives.
We will make the Spaniard promise, if we yield, to let us
      go;
We shall live to fight again and to strike another blow."
And the lion there lay dying, and they yielded to the foe.


And the stately Spanish men to their flagship bore him
      then,
Where they laid him by the mast, old Sir Richard caught
      at last,
And they praised him to his face with their courtly for-
      eign grace;
But he rose upon their decks, and he cried:
"I have fought for Queen and Faith like a valiant man
      and true;
I have only done my duty as a man is bound to do.
With a joyful spirit I Sir Richard Grenville die!"
And he fell upon their decks, and he died.


And they stared at the dead that had been so valiant and
      true,
And had holden the power and glory of Spain so cheap
That he dared her with one little ship and his English
      few;
Was he devil or man? He was devil for aught they knew,
But they sank his body with honor down into the deep,
And they manned the *Revenge* with a swarthier alien
      crew,
And away she sailed with her loss and longed for her
      own;

When a wind from the lands they had ruined awoke from
   sleep,
And the water began to heave and the weather to moan,
And or ever that evening ended a great gale blew,
And a wave like the wave that is raised by an earthquake
   grew,
Till it smote on their hulls and their sails and their masts
   and their flags,
And the whole sea plunged and fell on the shot-shattered
   navy of Spain,
And the little *Revenge* herself went down by the island
   crags
To be lost evermore in the main.

*Alfred Tennyson*

# Hervé Riel

### I

On the sea and at the Hogue, sixteen hundred ninety-
two,
  Did the English fight the French,—woe to France!
And, the thirty-first of May, helter-skelter through the
blue,
Like a crowd of frightened porpoises a shoal of sharks
pursue,
  Came crowding ship on ship to Saint Malo on the
Rance,
With the English fleet in view.

### II

'Twas the squadron that escaped, with the victor in full
chase;
  First and foremost of the drove, in his great ship,
Damfreville;
    Close on him fled, great and small,
    Twenty-two good ships in all;
  And they signalled to the place
  "Help the winners of a race!
    Get us guidance, give us harbor, take us quick—or,
quicker still,
    Here's the English can and will!"

### III

Then the pilots of the place put out brisk and leapt on
      board;
"Why, what hope or chance have ships like these to pass?"
      laughed they:
"Rocks to starboard, rocks to port, all the passage scarred
      and scored,
Shall the *Formidable* here, with her twelve-and-eighty
      guns,
  Think to make the river-mouth by the single narrow
      way,
Trust to enter where 'tis ticklish for a craft of twenty
      tons,
    And with flow at full beside?
    Now, 'tis slackest ebb of tide.
  Reach the mooring? Rather say,
While rock stands or water runs,
  Not a ship will leave the bay!"

### IV

Then was called a council straight.
Brief and bitter the debate:
"Here's the English at our heels; would you have them
    take in tow
All that's left us of the fleet, linked together stern and
    bow,
For a prize to Plymouth Sound?
Better run the ships aground!"
  (Ended Damfreville his speech).
"Not a minute more to wait!

Let the Captains all and each
Shove ashore, then blow up, burn the vessels on the
    beach!
France must undergo her fate.

V

"Give the word!" But no such word
Was ever spoke or heard;
    For up stood, for out stepped, for in struck amid all
      these
—A Captain? A Lieutenant? A Mate—first, second, third?
    No such man of mark, and meet
    With his betters to compete!
    But a simple Breton sailor pressed by Tourville for the
      fleet,
A poor coasting-pilot he, Hervé Riel the Croisickese.

VI

And "What mockery or malice have we here?" cries
    Hervé Riel:
"Are you mad, you Malouins? Are you cowards, fools, or
    rogues?
Talk to me of rocks and shoals, me who took the sound-
    ings, tell
On my fingers every bank, every shallow, every swell
    'Twixt the offing here and Grève where the river dis-
      embogues?
Are you bought by English gold? Is it love the lying's for?
    Morn and eve, night and day,
      Have I piloted your bay,

163

Entered free and anchored fast at the foot of Solidor.
   Burn the fleet and ruin France? That were worse than
      fifty Hogues!
      Sirs, they know I speak the truth! Sirs, believe me
      there's a way!
Only let me lead the line,
   Have the biggest ship to steer,
   Get this *Formidable* clear,
Make the others follow mine,
And I lead them, most and least, by a passage I know well,
   Right to Solidor past Grève,
      And there lay them safe and sound;
      And if one ship misbehave,—
         —Keel so much as grate the ground,
Why, I've nothing but my life,—here's my head!" cries
      Hervé Riel.


VII

Not a minute more to wait.
"Steer us in, then, small and great!
   Take the helm, lead the line, save the squadron!" cried
      its chief.
Captains, give the sailor place!
   He is Admiral, in brief.
Still the north-wind, by God's grace!
See the noble fellow's face
As the big ship, with a bound,
Clears the entry like a hound,
Keeps the passage, as its inch of way were the wide seas
      profound!

See, safe through shoal and rock,
  How they follow in a flock,
Not a ship that misbehaves, not a keel that grates the
    ground,
  Not a spar that comes to grief!
The peril, see, is past.
All are harbored to the last,
And just as Hervé Riel hollas "Anchor!"—sure as fate,
Up the English come,—too late!

VIII

So, the storm subsides to calm:
  They see the green trees wave
  On the heights o'erlooking Grève.
Hearts that bled are stanched with balm.
"Just our rapture to enhance,
  Let the English rake the bay,
Gnash their teeth and glare askance
  As they cannonade away!
'Neath rampired Solidor pleasant riding on the Rance!"
How hope succeeds despair on each Captain's counte-
    nance!
Out burst all with one accord,
  "This is Paradise for Hell!
  Let France, let France's King
  Thank the man that did the thing!"
What a shout, and all one word,
  "Hervé Riel!"
As he stepped in front once more,
  Not a symptom of surprise
  In the frank blue Breton eyes,
Just the same man as before.

## IX

Then said Damfreville, "My friend,
I must speak out at the end,
    Though I find the speaking hard.
Praise is deeper than the lips:
You have saved the King his ships,
    You must name your own reward.
'Faith, our sun was near eclipse!
Demand whate'er you will,
France remains your debtor still.
Ask to heart's content and have! or my name's not Dam-
    freville."

## X

Then a beam of fun outbroke
On the bearded mouth that spoke,
As the honest heart laughed through
Those frank eyes of Breton blue:
"Since I needs must say my say,
    Since on board the duty's done,
    And from Malo Roads to Croisic Point, what is it but a
        run?—
Since 'tis ask and have, I may—
    Since the others go ashore—
Come! A good whole holiday!
    Leave to go and see my wife, whom I call the Belle
        Aurore!"
    That he asked and that he got,—nothing more.

## XI

Name and deed alike are lost:
Not a pillar or a post
    In his Croisic keeps alive the feat as it befell;
Not a head in white and black
On a single fishing-smack,
In memory of the man but for whom had gone to wrack
    All that France saved from the fight whence England
        bore the bell:
Go to Paris: rank on rank
    Search the heroes flung pell-mell
On the Louvre, face and flank!
    You shall look long enough ere you come to Hervé
        Riel.
So, for better and for worse,
Hervé Riel, accept my verse!
In my verse, Hervé Riel, do thou once more
Save the squadron, honor France, love thy wife the Belle
        Aurore!

*Robert Browning*

# An Old-Time Sea-Fight

Would you hear of an old-time sea-fight?
Would you learn who won by the light of the moon and
    stars?
List to the yarn, as my grandmother's father the sailor
    told it to me.

Our foe was no skulk in his ship I tell you (said he),
His was the surly English pluck, and there is no tougher
    or truer, and never was and never will be;
Along the lower'd eve he came horribly raking us.

We closed with him, the yards entangled, the cannon
    touch'd,
My captain lash'd fast with his own hands.

We had receiv'd some eighteen pound shots under the
    water,
On our lower-gun-deck two large pieces had burst at the
    first fire, killing all around and blowing up over-
    head.

Fighting at sun-down, fighting at dark,
Ten o'clock at night, the full moon well up, our leaks on
    the gain, and five feet of water reported,

The master-at-arms loosing the prisoners confined in the
    afterhold to give them a chance for themselves.


The transit to and from the magazine is now stopt by the
    sentinels,
They see so many strange faces they do not know whom to
    trust.


Our frigate takes fire,
The other asks if we demand quarter?
If our colours are struck and the fighting done?


Now I laugh content, for I hear the voice of my little
    captain,
*We have not struck,* he composedly cries, *we have just be-
    gun our part of the fighting.*


Only three guns are in use,
One is directed by the captain himself against the enemy's
    main-mast,
Two well serv'd with grape and canister silence his mus-
    ketry and clear his decks.


The tops alone second the fire of this little battery, espe-
    cially the main-top,
They hold out bravely during the whole of the action.


Not a moment's cease,
The leaks gain fast on the pumps, the fire eats toward the
    powder-magazine.

One of the pumps has been shot away, it is generally
thought we are sinking.

Serene stands the little captain,
He is not hurried, his voice is neither high nor low,
His eyes give more light to us than our battle-lanterns.

Toward twelve there in the beams of the moon they surrender to us.

*Walt Whitman*
*from "Song of Myself"*

# Hohenlinden

(DECEMBER 3, 1800)

On Linden, when the sun was low,
All bloodless lay the untrodden snow;
And dark as winter was the flow
    Of Iser, rolling rapidly.

But Linden saw another sight,
When the drum beat, at dead of night,
Commanding fires of death to light
    The darkness of her scenery.

By torch and trumpet fast arrayed
Each horseman drew his battle-blade,
And furious every charger neighed
    To join the dreadful revelry.

Then shook the hills with thunder riven;
Then rushed the steed, to battle driven;
And louder than the bolts of heaven
    Far flashed the red artillery.

But redder yet that light shall glow
On Linden's hills of stainèd snow;
And bloodier yet the torrent flow
    Of Iser, rolling rapidly.

'Tis morn; but scarce yon level sun
Can pierce the war-clouds, rolling dun,
Where furious Frank and fiery Hun
    Shout in their sulphurous canopy.

The combat deepens. On, ye Brave,
Who rush to glory, or the grave!
Wave, Munich! all thy banners wave,
    And charge with all thy chivalry!

Few, few shall part, where many meet!
The snow shall be their winding-sheet,
And every turf beneath their feet
    Shall be a soldier's sepulchre.

*Thomas Campbell*

# The Defence of the Alamo

(MARCH 6, 1836)

Santa Ana came storming, as a storm might come;
   There was rumble of cannon; there was rattle of glade;
There was cavalry, infantry, bugle and drum,—
   Full seven thousand, in pomp and parade,
The chivalry, flower of Mexico;
And a gaunt two hundred in the Alamo!

And thirty lay sick, and some were shot through;
   For the siege had been bitter, and bloody, and long.
"Surrender, or die!"—"Men, what will *you* do?"
   And Travis, great Travis, drew sword, quick and
      strong;
Drew a line at his feet . . . "Will you come? Will you go?
*I* die with my wounded, in the Alamo."

Then Bowie gasped, "Lead me over that line!"
   Then Crockett, one hand to the sick, one hand to his
      gun,
Crossed with him; then never a word or a sign
   Till all, sick or well, all, all save but one,
One man. Then a woman stepped, praying, and slow
Across; to die at her post in the Alamo.

Then that one coward fled, in the night, in that night
  When all men silently prayed and thought
Of home; of to-morrow; of God and the right,
  Till dawn: and with dawn came Travis's cannon-shot
In answer to insolent Mexico,
From the old bell-tower of the Alamo.

Then came Santa Ana; a crescent of flame!
  Then the red escalade; then the fight hand to hand;
Such an unequal fight as never had name
  Since the Persian hordes butchered that doomed Spartan band.
All day—all day and all night; and the morning? so slow,
Through the battle-smoke mantling the Alamo.

Now silence! Such silence! Two thousand lay dead
  In a crescent outside! And within? Not a breath
Save the gasp of a woman, with gory gashed head,
  All alone, all alone there, waiting for death;
And she but a nurse. Yet when shall we know
Another like this of the Alamo?

Shout "Victory, victory, victory ho!"
  I say 'tis not always to the hosts that win!
I say that the victory, high or low,
  Is given the hero who grapples with sin,
Or legion or single; just asking to know
When duty fronts death in his Alamo.

*Joaquin Miller*

174

# How Old Brown Took Harper's Ferry

(OCTOBER 16, 1859)

John Brown in Kansas settled, like a steadfast Yankee
    farmer,
  Grave and godly, with four sons, all stalwart men of
    might.
There he spoke aloud for freedom, and the Border-strife
    grew warmer,
  Till the Rangers fired his dwelling, in his absence, in
    the night;
            And Old Brown,
            Osawatomie Brown,
Came homeward in the morning—to find his house
  burned down.
Then he grasped his trusty rifle and boldly fought for
    freedom;
  Smote from border unto border the fierce, invading
    band;
And he and his brave boys vowed—so might Heaven help
    and speed em!—
  They would save those grand old prairies from the
    curse that blights the land;
            And Old Brown,
            Osawatomie Brown,

Said, "Boys, the Lord will aid us!" and he shoved his ram-
rod down.

And the Lord *did* aid these men, and they labored day and
even,
Saving Kansas from its peril; and their very lives seemed
charmed,
Till the ruffians killed one son, in the blessed light of
Heaven:
In cold blood the fellows slew him, as he journeyed all
unarmed;
Then Old Brown,
Osawatomie Brown,
Shed not a tear, but shut his teeth, and frowned a terrible
frown!

Then they seized another brave boy,—not amid the heat
of battle,
But in peace, behind his ploughshare,—and they
loaded him with chains,
And with pikes, before their horses, even as they goad
their cattle,
Drove him cruelly, for their sport, and at last blew out
his brains;
Then Old Brown,
Osawatomie Brown,
Raised his right hand up to Heaven, calling Heaven's
vengeance down.

And he swore a fearful oath, by the name of the Almighty,
He would hunt this ravening evil that had scathed and
torn him so;

He would seize it by the vitals; he would crush it day and
 night; he
 Would so pursue its footsteps, so return it blow for
  blow,
    That Old Brown,
    Osawatomie Brown,
Should be a name to swear by, in backwoods or in town!

Then his beard became more grizzled, and his wild blue
 eye grew wilder,
 And more sharply curved his hawk's-nose, snuffing battle from afar;
And he and the two boys left, though the Kansas strife
 waxed milder,
 Grew more sullen, till was over the bloody Border War,
    And Old Brown,
    Osawatomie Brown,
Had gone crazy, as they reckoned by his fearful glare and
 frown.

So, he left the plains of Kansas and their bitter woes behind him,
 Slipped off into Virginia, where the statesmen all are
  born.
Hired a farm by Harper's Ferry, and no one knew where
 to find him,
 Or whether he'd turned parson, or was jacketed and
  shorn;
    For Old Brown,
    Osawatomie Brown,
Mad as he was, knew texts enough to wear a parson's
 gown.

177

He bought no ploughs and harrows, spades and shovels,
    and such trifles;
  But quietly to his rancho there came, by every train,
Boxes full of pikes and pistols, and his well-beloved
    Sharp's rifles;
  And eighteen other madmen joined their leader there
    again.
             Says Old Brown,
             Osawatomie Brown,
"Boys, we've got an army large enough to march and take
    the town!

"Take the town, and seize the muskets, free the negroes,
    and then arm them;
  Carry the County and the State, ay, and all the potent
    South.
On their own heads be the slaughter, if their victims rise
    to harm them—
  These Virginians! who believed not, nor would heed
    the warning mouth."
             Says Old Brown,
             Osawatomie Brown,
"The world shall see a Republic, or my name is not John
    Brown."

'Twas the sixteenth of October, on the evening of a
    Sunday:
  "This good work," declared the captain, "shall be on a
    holy night!"
It was on a Sunday evening, and before the noon of Mon-
    day,

With two sons, and Captain Stephens, fifteen privates—
 black and white,
> Captain Brown,
> Osawatomie Brown,
Marched across the bridged Potomac, and knocked the
 sentry down;

Took the guarded armory-building, and the muskets and
 the cannon;
 Captured all the county majors and colonels, one by
 one;
Scared to death each gallant scion of Virginia they ran on,
 And before the noon of Monday, I say, the deed was
 done.
> Mad Old Brown,
> Osawatomie Brown,
With his eighteen other crazy men, went in and took the
 town.

Very little noise and bluster, little smell of powder made
 he;
 It was all done in the midnight, like the Emperor's
 *coup d'état*.
"Cut the wires! Stop the rail-cars! Hold the streets and
 bridges!" said he,
 Then declared the new Republic, with himself for guid-
 ing star,—
> This Old Brown,
> Osawatomie Brown,
And the bold two thousand citizens ran off and left the
 town.

Then was riding and railroading and expressing here and
    thither;
  And the Martinsburg Sharpshooters and the Charles-
    town Volunteers,
And the Shepherdstown and Winchester Militia hastened
    whither
  Old Brown was said to muster his ten thousand grena-
    diers.
                General Brown!
                Osawatomie Brown!
Behind whose rampant banner all the North was pouring
    down.

But at last, 'tis said, some prisoners escaped from Old
    Brown's durance,
  And the effervescent valor of the Chivalry broke out,
When they learned that nineteen madmen had the mar-
    vellous assurance—
  Only nineteen—thus to seize the place and drive them
    straight about;
                And Old Brown,
                Osawatomie Brown,
Found an army come to take him, encamped around the
    town.

But to storm, with all the forces I have mentioned, was
    too risky;
  So they hurried off to Richmond for the Government
    Marines,
Tore them from their weeping matrons, fired their souls
    with Bourbon whiskey,

Till they battered down Brown's castle with their lad-
    ders and machines;
                And Old Brown,
                Osawatomie Brown,
Received three bayonet stabs, and a cut on his brave old
    crown.


Tallyho! the old Virginia gentry gather to the baying!
    In they rushed and killed the game, shooting lustily
        away;
And whene'er they slew a rebel, those who came too late
    for slaying,
    Not to lose a share of glory, fired their bullets in his
        clay;
                And Old Brown,
                Osawatomie Brown,
Saw his sons fall dead beside him, and between them laid
    him down.


How the conquerors wore their laurels; how they has-
    tened on the trial;
    How Old Brown was placed, half dying, on the Charles-
    town court-house floor;
How he spoke his grand oration, in the scorn of all denial;
    What the brave old madman told them,—these are
    known the country o'er.
                "Hang Old Brown,
                Osawatomie Brown,"
Said the judge, "and all such rebels!" with his most judi-
    cial frown.

But, Virginians, don't do it! for I tell you that the flagon,
  Filled with blood of Old Brown's offspring, was first
    poured by Southern hands;
And each drop from Old Brown's life-veins, like the red
    gore of the dragon,
  May spring up a vengeful Fury, hissing through your
    slave-worn lands!
        And Old Brown,
        Osawatomie Brown,
May trouble you more than ever, when you've nailed his
  coffin down!

*Edmund Clarence Stedman*

# Custer's Last Charge

(JUNE 25, 1876)

Dead! Is it possible? He, the bold rider,
    Custer, our hero, the first in the fight,
Charming the bullets of yore to fly wider,
    Far from our battle-king's ringlets of light!
Dead, our young chieftain, and dead, all forsaken!
    No one to tell us the way of his fall!
Slain in the desert, and never to waken,
    Never, not even to victory's call!

Proud for his fame that last day that he met them!
    All the night long he had been on their track,
Scorning their traps and the men that had set them,
    Wild for a charge that should never give back.
There on the hilltop he halted and saw them.—
    Lodges all loosened and ready to fly;
Hurrying scouts with the tidings to awe them,
    Told of his coming before he was nigh.

All the wide valley was full of their forces,
    Gathered to cover the lodges' retreat!—
Warriors running in haste to their horses,
    Thousands of enemies close to his feet!

Down in the valleys the ages had hollowed,
　　There lay the Sitting Bull's camp for a prey!
Numbers! What recked he? What recked those who fol-
　　　　lowed—
　　Men who had fought ten to one ere that day?

Out swept the squadrons, the fated three hundred,
　　Into the battle-line steady and full;
Then down the hillside exultingly thundered,
　　Into the hordes of the old Sitting Bull!
Wild Ogalallah, Arapahoe, Cheyenne,
　　Wild Horse's braves, and the rest of their crew,
Shrank from that charge like a herd from a lion,—
　　Then closed around, the grim horde of wild Sioux!

Right to their center he charged, and then facing—
　　Hark to those yells! and around them, O see!
Over the hilltops the Indians come racing,
　　Coming as fast as the waves of the sea!
Red was the circle of fire around them;
　　No hope of victory, no ray of light,
Shot through that terrible black cloud without them,
　　Brooding in death over Custer's last fight.

Then did he blench? Did he die like a craven,
　　Begging those torturing fiends for his life?
Was there a soldier who carried the Seven
　　Flinched like a coward or fled from the strife?
No, by the blood of our Custer, no quailing!
　　There in the midst of the Indians they close,
Hemmed in by thousands, but ever assailing,
　　Fighting like tigers, all bayed amid foes!

Thicker and thicker the bullets came singing;
   Down go the horses and riders and all;
Swiftly the warriors round them were ringing,
   Circling like buzzards awaiting their fall.
See the wild steeds of the mountain and prairie,
   Savage eyes gleaming from forests of mane;
Quivering lances with pennons so airy
   War-painted warriors charging amain.

Backward, again and again, they were driven,
   Shrinking to close with the lost little band;
Never a cap that had worn the bright Seven
   Bowed till its wearer was dead on the strand.
Closer and closer the death-circle growing,
   Ever the leader's voice, clarion clear,
Rang out his words of encouragement glowing,
   "We can but die once, boys,—we'll sell our lives dear!"

Dearly they sold them like Berserkers raging,
   Facing the death that encircled them round;
Death's bitter pangs by their vengeance assuaging,
   Marking their tracks by their dead on the ground.
Comrades, our children shall yet tell their story,—
   Custer's last charge on the old Sitting Bull;
And ages shall swear that the cup of his glory
   Needed but that death to render it full.

*Frederick Whittaker*

# Rogues and Heroes

# The Lincolnshire Poacher

When I was bound apprentice, in famous Lincolnshire,
Full well I served my master for more than seven year,
Till I took up to poaching, as you shall quickly hear:
Oh, 'tis my delight on a shining night, in the season of the
    year.

As me and my companions were setting of a snare,
'Twas then we spied the game-keeper, for him we did not
    care.
For we can wrestle and fight, my boys, and jump out any
    where;
Oh, 'tis my delight on a shining night, in the season of the
    year.

As me and my companions were setting four or five,
And, taking on 'em up again, we caught a hare alive.
We took the hare alive, my boys, and through the wood
    did steer:
Oh, 'tis my delight on a shining night, in the season of the
    year.

I threw him on my shoulder, and then we trudgèd home,
We took him to a neighbour's house and sold him for a
    crown,

THE LINCOLNSHIRE POACHER

We sold him for a crown, my boys, but I did not tell you
　　where:
Oh, 'tis my delight on a shining night, in the season of the
　　year.

Success to every gentleman that lives in Lincolnshire,
Success to every poacher that wants to sell a hare,
Bad luck to every game-keeper that will not sell his deer:
Oh, 'tis my delight on a shining night, in the season of the
　　year.

*Traditional: English*

# The Land

('Friendly Brook'—*A Diversity of Creatures*)


When Julius Fabricius, Sub-Prefect of the Weald,
In the days of Diocletian owned our Lower River-field,
He called to him Hobdenius—a Briton of the Clay,
Saying: 'What about that River-piece for layin' in to hay?'

And the aged Hobden answered: 'I remember as a lad
My father told your father that she wanted dreenin' bad.
An' the more that you neglect her the less you'll get her
    clean.
Have it jest *as* you've a mind to, but, if I was you, I'd
    dreen.'

So they drained it long and crossways in the lavish Roman
    style—
Still we find among the river-drift their flakes of ancient
    tile,
And in drouthy middle August, when the bones of mead-
    ows show,
We can trace the lines they followed sixteen hundred
    years ago.

When Julius Fabricius died as even Prefects do,
And after certain centuries, Imperial Rome died too.

Then did robbers enter Britain from across the Northern
    main
And our River-field was won by Ogier the Dane.

Well could Ogier work his war-boat—well could Ogier
    wield his brand—
Much he knew of foaming waters—not so much of farm-
    ing land.
So he called to him a Hobden of the old unaltered blood,
Saying: 'What about that River-piece; she doesn't look no
    good?'

And that aged Hobden answered: ' 'Tain't for *me* to inter-
    terfere,
But I've known that bit o' meadow now for five and fifty
    year.
Have it *jest* as you've a mind to, but I've proved it time on
    time,
If you want to change her nature you have *got* to give her
    lime!'

Ogier sent his wains to Lewes, twenty hours' solemn walk,
And drew back great abundance of the cool, grey, healing
    chalk,
And old Hobden spread it broadcast, never heeding what
    was in't.—
Which is why in cleaning ditches, now and then we find a
    flint.

Ogier died. His sons grew English—Anglo-Saxon was
    their name—
Till out of blossomed Normandy another pirate came;

For Duke William conquered England and divided with
    his men,
And our Lower River-field he gave to William of War-
    enne.

But the Brook (you know her habit) rose one rainy au-
    tumn night
And tore down sodden flitches of the bank to left and
    right.
So, said William to his Bailiff as they rode their dripping
    rounds:
'Hob, what about that River-bit—the Brook's got up no
    bounds?'

And that aged Hobden answered: ' 'Tain't my business to
    advise,
But ye might ha' known 'twould happen from the way the
    valley lies.
Where ye can't hold back the water you must try and save
    the sile.
Hev it jest as you've a *mind* to, but, if I was you, I'd spile!'

They spiled along the water-course with trunks of willow-
    trees,
And planks of elms behind 'em and immortal oaken
    knees.
And when the spates of Autumn whirl the gravel-beds
    away
You can see their faithful fragments, iron-hard in iron
    clay.

\*    \*    \*    \*    \*

*Georgii Quinti Anno Sexto,* I, who own the River-field,
Am fortified with title-deeds, attested, signed and sealed,
Guaranteeing me, my assigns, my executors and heirs
All sorts of powers and profits which—are neither mine
     nor theirs.

I have rights of chase and warren, as my dignity requires.
I can fish—but Hobden tickles. I can shoot—but Hobden
     wires.
I repair, but he reopens, certain gaps which, men allege,
Have been used by every Hobden since a Hobden
     swapped a hedge.

Shall I dog his morning progress o'er the track-betraying
     dew?
Demand his dinner-basket into which my pheasant flew?
Confiscate his evening faggot under which my conies ran,
And summons him to judgment? I would sooner summons
     Pan.

His dead are in the churchyard—thirty generations laid.
Their names were old in history when Domesday Book
     was made;
And the passion and the piety and prowess of his line
Have seeded, rooted, fruited in some land the Law calls
     mine.

Not for any beast that burrows, not for any bird that flies,
Would I lose his large sound counsel, miss his keen
  amending eyes.
He is bailiff, woodman, wheelwright, field-surveyor, en-
  gineer,
And if flagrantly a poacher—'tain't for me to interfere.

'Hob, what about that River-bit?' I turn to him again,
With Fabricius and Ogier and William of Warenne.
'Hev it jest as you've a mind to, *but*'—and here he takes
  command.
For whoever pays the taxes old Mus' Hobden owns the
  land.

*Rudyard Kipling*

# The War-Song of Dinas Vawr

The mountain sheep are sweeter,
But the valley sheep are fatter;
We therefore deemed it meeter
To carry off the latter.
We made an expedition;
We met a host, and quelled it;
We forced a strong position,
And killed the men who held it.

On Dyfed's richest valley,
Where herds of kine were browsing,
We made a mighty sally,
To furnish our carousing.
Fierce warriors rushed to meet us;
We met them, and o'erthrew them:
They struggled hard to beat us;
But we conquered them, and slew them.

As we drove our prize at leisure,
The king marched forth to catch us:
His rage surpassed all measure,
But his people could not match us.
He fled to his hall-pillars;
And, ere our force we led off,

Some sacked his house and cellars,
While others cut his head off.

We there, in strife bewild'ring,
Spilt blood enough to swim in:
We orphaned many children,
And widowed many women.
The eagles and the ravens
We glutted with our foemen;
The heroes and the cravens,
The spearmen and the bowmen.

We brought away from battle,
And much their land bemoaned them,
Two thousand head of cattle,
And the head of him who owned them:
Ednyfed, king of Dyfed,
His head was borne before us;
His wine and beasts supplied our feasts,
And his overthrow, our chorus.

*Thomas Love Peacock*

# Forty Singing Seamen

"In our lands be Beeres and Lyons of dyvers colours as ye redd, grene, black, and white. And in our land be also unicornes and these Unicornes slee many Lyons. . . . Also there dare no man make a lye in our lande, for if he dyde he sholde incontynent be sleyn."—*Mediaeval Epistle, of Pope Prester John.*

Across the seas of Wonderland to Mogadore we plodded,
    Forty singing seamen in an old black barque,
And we landed in the twilight where a Polyphemus
        nodded
    With his battered moon-eye winking red and yellow
        through the dark!
            For his eye was growing mellow,
            Rich and ripe and red and yellow,
    As was time, since old Ulysses made him bellow in the
        dark!
Cho.—Since Ulysses bunged his eye up with a pine-torch
        in the dark!

II

*Were* they mountains in the gloaming or the giant's ugly
        shoulders
    Just beneath the rolling eyeball, with its bleared and
        vinous glow,

Red and yellow o'er the purple of the pines among the
    boulders
    And the shaggy horror brooding on the sullen slopes
      below,
        *Were* they pines among the boulders
        Or the hair upon his shoulders?
We were only simple seamen, so of course we didn't
    know.
*Cho.*—We were simple singing seamen, so of course we
    couldn't know.

### III

But we crossed a plain of poppies, and we came upon a
    fountain
    Not of water, but of jewels, like a spray of leaping fire;
And behind it, in an emerald glade, beneath a golden
    mountain
    There stood a crystal palace, for a sailor to admire;
        For a troop of ghosts came round us,
        Which with leaves of bay they crowned us,
    Then with grog they well nigh drowned us, to the depth
    of our desire!
*Cho.*—And 'twas very friendly of them, as a sailor can
    admire!

### IV

There was music all about us, we were growing quite
    forgetful
    We were only singing seamen from the dirt of London-
    town,

Though the nectar that we swallowed seemed to vanish
    half regretful
  As if we wasn't good enough to take such vittles down,
      When we saw a sudden figure,
      Tall and black as any nigger,
  Like the devil—only bigger—drawing near us with a
    frown!
*Cho.*—Like the devil—but much bigger—and he wore a
    golden crown!


## V

And "What's all this?" he growls at us! With dignity we
    chaunted
  "Forty singing seamen, sir, as won't be put upon!"
"What? Englishmen?" he cries, "Well, if ye don't mind
    being haunted,
    Faith you're welcome to my palace; I'm the famous
    Prester John!
        Will ye walk into my palace?
        I don't bear 'ee any malice!
    One and all ye shall be welcome in the halls of Prester
    John!"
*Cho.*—So we walked into the palace and the halls of
    Prester John!


## VI

Now the door was one great diamond and the hall a hol-
    low ruby—
  Big as Beachy Head, my lads, nay bigger by a half!

And I sees the mate wi' mouth agape, a-staring like a
  booby,
  And the skipper close behind him, with his tongue out
    like a calf!
      Now the way to take it rightly
      Was to walk along politely
  Just as if you didn't notice—so I couldn't help but
    laugh!
Cho.—For they both forgot their manners and the crew
  was bound to laugh!


## VII

But he took us through his palace and, my lads, as I'm a
  sinner,
  We walked into an opal like a sunset-coloured cloud—
"My dining-room," he says, and, quick as light we saw a
  dinner
  Spread before us by the fingers of a hidden fairy crowd;
      And the skipper, swaying gently
      After dinner, murmurs faintly,
  "I looks to-wards you, Prester John, you've done us very
    proud!"
Cho.—And we drank his health with honours, for he *done*
  us *very* proud!


## VIII

Then he walks us to his garden where we sees a feathered
  demon
  Very splendid and important on a sort of spicy tree!

"That's the Phoenix," whispers Prester, "which all eddi-
cated seamen
　Knows the only one existent, and *he's* waiting for to
　flee!
　　　When his hundred years expire
　　　Then he'll set hisself a-fire
　And another from his ashes rise most beautiful to see!"
*Cho.*—With wings of rose and emerald most beautiful to
　see!


IX

Then he says, "In younder forest there's a little silver
river,
　And whosoever drinks of it, his youth shall never die!
The centuries go by, but Prester John endures for ever
　With his music in the mountains and his magic on the
　sky!
　　　While *your* hearts are growing colder,
　　　While your world is growing older,
　There's a magic in the distance, where the sea-line
　meets the sky."
*Cho.*—It shall call to singing seamen till the fount o' song
　is dry!


X

So we thought we'd up and seek it, but that forest fair
defied us,—
　First a crimson leopard laughs at us most horrible to
　see,

Then a sea-green lion came and sniffed and licked his
    chops and eyed us,
  While a red and yellow unicorn was dancing round a
    tree!
       *We* was trying to look thinner,
       Which was hard, because our dinner
Must ha' made us very tempting to a cat o' high degree!
*Cho.*—Must ha' made us very tempting to the whole
    manarjeree!

### XI

So we scuttled from that forest and across the poppy
    meadows
  Where the awful shaggy horror brooded o'er us in the
    dark!
And we pushes out from shore again a-jumping at our
    shadows,
  And pulls away most joyful to the old black barque!
       And home again we plodded
       While the Polyphemus nodded
  With his battered moon-eye winking red and yellow
    through the dark.
*Cho.*—Oh, the moon above the mountains, red and yellow
    through the dark!

### XII

Across the seas of Wonderland to London-town we blun-
    dered,
  Forty singing seamen as was puzzled for to know

If the visions that we saw was caused by—here again we
    pondered—
A tipple in a vision forty thousand years ago.
      Could the grog we *dreamt* we swallowed
      Make us *dream* of all that followed?
We were only simple seamen, so of course we didn't
    know!
*Cho.*—We were simple singing seamen, so of course we
    could not know!

*Alfred Noyes*

# Derelict

A REMINISCENCE OF "TREASURE ISLAND"
(CAP'N BILLY BONES HIS SONG)

Fifteen men on the dead man's chest—
    Yo-ho-ho and a bottle of rum!
Drink and the devil had done for the rest—
    Yo-ho-ho and a bottle of rum!
The mate was fixed by the bos'n's pike,
The bos'n brained with a marlinspike.
      It had been gripped
        By fingers ten;
      And there they lay,
        All good dead men,
Like break-o'-day in a boozing-ken—
    Yo-ho-ho and a bottle of rum!


Fifteen men of a whole ship's list—
    Yo-ho-ho and a bottle of rum!
All of 'em down from the devil's own fist—
    Yo-ho-ho and a bottle of rum!
The skipper lay with his nob in gore
Where the scullion's axe his cheek had shore—
And the scullion he was stabbed times four.

And there they lay,
  And the soggy skies
Dripped all day long
  In up-staring eyes—
At murk sunset and at foul sunrise—
  Yo-ho-ho and a bottle of rum!


Fifteen men of 'em stiff and stark—
  Yo-ho-ho and a bottle of rum!
Ten of the crew had the murder mark—
  Yo-ho-ho and a bottle of rum!
'Twas a cutlass swipe, or an ounce of lead,
Or a yawing hole in a battered head—
And the scuppers glut with a rotting red.
  And there they lay,
    Aye, damn my eyes!—
  All lookouts clapped
  On paradise—
All souls bound just contrariwise—
  Yo-ho-ho and a bottle of rum!


Fifteen men of 'em good and true—
  Yo-ho-ho and a bottle of rum!
Every man jack could ha' sailed with old **Pew**—
  Yo-ho-ho and a bottle of rum!
There was chest on chest full of Spanish gold,
With a ton of plate in the middle hold,
And the cabins riot of stuff untold,

And they lay there
  That had took the plum,
With sightless glare
  And their lips struck dumb,
While we shared all by the rule of thumb—
  Yo-ho-ho and a bottle of rum!

Fifteen men on the dead man's chest—
  Yo-ho-ho and a bottle of rum!
Drink and the devil had done for the rest—
  Yo-ho-ho and a bottle of rum!
We wrapped 'em all in a mains'l tight,
With twice ten turns of the hawser's bight,
And we heaved 'em over and out of sight—
    With a yo-heave-ho!
    And a fare-you-well!
    And a sullen plunge
    In the sullen swell
Ten fathoms deep on the road to hell—
  Yo-ho-ho and a bottle of rum!

                    *Young E. Allison*

# Spanish Waters

Spanish waters, Spanish waters, you are ringing in my ears,
Like a slow sweet piece of music from the grey forgotten
    years;
Telling tales, and beating tunes, and bringing weary
    thoughts to me
Of the sandy beach at Muertos, where I would that I could
    be.


There's a surf breaks on Los Muertos, and it never stops
    to roar,
And it's there we came to anchor, and it's there we went
    ashore,
Where the blue lagoon is silent amid snags of rotting trees,
Dropping like the clothes of corpses cast up by the seas.


We anchored at Los Muertos when the dipping sun was
    red,
We left her half-a-mile to sea, to west of Nigger Head;
And before the mist was on the Cay, before the day was
    done,
We were all ashore on Muertos with the gold that we had
    won.

We bore it through the marshes in a half-score battered
  chests,
Sinking, in the sucking quagmires, to the sunburn on our
  breasts,
Heaving over tree-trunks, gasping, damning at the flies
  and heat,
Longing for a long drink, out of silver, in the ship's cool
  lazareet.\*

The moon came white and ghostly as we laid the treasure
  down,
There was gear there'd make a beggarman as rich as Lima
  Town,
Copper charms and silver trinkets from the chests of Span-
  ish crews,
Gold doubloons and double moydores, louis d'ors and
  portagues,†

Clumsy yellow-metal earrings from the Indians of Brazil,
Uncut emeralds out of Rio, bezoar stones from Guaya-
  quil;
Silver, in the crude and fashioned, pots of old Arica
  bronze,
Jewels from the bones of Incas desecrated by the Dons.

We smoothed the place with mattocks, and we took and
  blazed the tree,
Which marks yon where the gear is hid that none will ever
  see,

\* Lazareet, or lazarette: a space between decks.
† Doubloons, moydores, louis d'ors, portagues: gold coins.

And we laid aboard the ship again, and south away we
    steers,
Through the loud surf of Los Muertos which is beating in
    my ears.

I'm the last alive that knows it. All the rest have gone
    their ways,
Killed, or died, or come to anchor in the old Mulatas
    Cays,
And I go singing, fiddling, old and starved and in despair,
And I know where all that gold is hid, if I were only there.

It's not the way to end it all. I'm old, and nearly blind,
And an old man's past's a strange thing, for it never leaves
    his mind.
And I see in dreams, awhiles, the beach, the sun's disc dip-
    ping red,
And the tall ship, under topsails, swaying in past Nigger
    Head.

I'd be glad to step ashore there. Glad to take a pick and go
To the lone blazed coco-palm tree in the place no others
    know,
And lift the gold and silver that has mouldered there for
    years
By the loud surf of Los Muertos which is beating in my
    ears.

*John Masefield*

# The Vision of Sir Launfal

Over his keys the musing organist,
   Beginning doubtfully and far away,
First lets his fingers wander as they list,
   And builds a bridge from Dreamland for his lay:
Then, as the touch of his loved instrument
   Gives hope and fervor, nearer draws his theme,
First guessed by faint auroral flushes sent
   Along the wavering vista of his dream.


      Not only around our infancy
      Doth heaven with all its splendors lie;
      Daily, with souls that cringe and plot,
      We Sinais climb and know it not.


Over our manhood bend the skies;
   Against our fallen and traitor lives
The great winds utter prophecies;
   With our faint hearts the mountain strives;
Its arms outstretched, the druid wood
   Waits with its benedicite;
And to our age's drowsy blood
   Still shouts the inspiring sea.

Earth gets its price for what Earth gives us;
   The beggar is taxed for a corner to die in,
The priest hath his fee who comes and shrives us,
   We bargain for the graves we lie in;
At the devil's booth are all things sold,
Each ounce of dross costs its ounce of gold;
   For a cap and bells our lives we pay,
Bubbles we buy with a whole soul's tasking:
   'T is heaven alone that is given away,
'T is only God may be had for the asking;
No price is set on the lavish summer;
June may be had by the poorest comer.

And what is so rare as a day in June?
   Then, if ever, come perfect days;
Then Heaven tries earth if it be in tune,
   And over it softly her warm ear lays:
Whether we look, or whether we listen,
We hear life murmur, or see it glisten;
Every clod feels a stir of might,
   An instinct within it that reaches and towers,
And, groping blindly above it for light,
   Climbs to a soul in grass and flowers;
The flush of life may well be seen
   Thrilling back over hills and valleys;
The cowslip startles in meadows green,
   The buttercup catches the sun in its chalice,
And there's never a leaf nor a blade too mean
   To be some happy creature's palace;
The little bird sits at his door in the sun,
   Atilt like a blossom among the leaves,

And lets his illumined being o'errun
   With the deluge of summer it receives;
His mate feels the eggs beneath her wings,
And the heart in her dumb breast flutters and sings;
He sings to the wide world, and she to her nest,—
In the nice ear of Nature which song is the best?


Now is the high-tide of the year,
   And whatever of life hath ebbed away
Comes flooding back with a ripply cheer,
   Into every bare inlet and creek and bay;
Now the heart is so full that a drop overfills it,
We are happy now because God wills it;
No matter how barren the past may have been,
'T is enough for us now that the leaves are green;
We sit in the warm shade and feel right well
How the sap creeps up and the blossoms swell;
We may shut our eyes, but we cannot help knowing
That skies are clear and grass is growing;
The breeze comes whispering in our ear,
That dandelions are blossoming near,
   That maize has sprouted, that streams are flowing,
That the river is bluer than the sky,
That the robin is plastering his house hard by;
And if the breeze kept the good news back,
For other couriers we should not lack;
   We could guess it all by yon heifer's lowing,—
And hark! how clear bold chanticleer,
Warmed with the new wine of the year,
   Tells all in his lusty crowing!

Joy comes, grief goes, we know not how;
Everything is happy now,
  Everything is upward striving;
'T is as easy now for the heart to be true
As for grass to be green or skies to be blue,—
  'T is the natural way of living:
Who knows whither the clouds have fled?
  In the unscarred heaven they leave no wake;
And the eyes forget the tears they have shed,
  The heart forgets its sorrow and ache;
The soul partakes the season's youth,
  And the sulphurous rifts of passion and woe
Lie deep 'neath a silence pure and smooth,
  Like burnt-out craters healed with snow.
What wonder if Sir Launfal now
Remembered the keeping of his vow?


PART FIRST

I

"My golden spurs now bring to me,
  And bring to me my richest mail,
For to-morrow I go over land and sea
  In search of the Holy Grail;
Shall never a bed for me be spread,
Nor shall a pillow be under my head,
Till I begin my vow to keep;
Here on the rushes will I sleep,
And perchance there may come a vision true
Ere day create the world anew."
  Slowly Sir Launfal's eyes grew dim,

Slumber fell like a cloud on him,
And into his soul the vision flew.

## II

The crows flapped over by twos and threes,
In the pool drowsed the cattle up to their knees.
  The little birds sang as if it were
  The one day of summer in all the year,
And the very leaves seemed to sing on the trees:
The castle alone in the landscape lay
Like an outpost of winter, dull and gray:
'T was the proudest hall in the North Countree,
And never its gates might opened be,
Save to lord or lady of high degree;
Summer besieged it on every side,
But the churlish stone her assaults defied;
She could not scale the chilly wall,
Though around it for leagues her pavilions tall
Stretched left and right,
Over the hills and out of sight;
  Green and broad was every tent,
  And out of each a murmur went
Till the breeze fell off at night.

## III

The drawbridge dropped with a surly clang,
And through the dark arch a charger sprang,
Bearing Sir Launfal, the maiden knight,
In his gilded mail, that flamed so bright
It seemed the dark castle had gathered all
Those shafts the fierce sun had shot over its wall

In his siege of three hundred summers long,
And, binding them all in one blazing sheaf,
  Had cast them forth: so, young and strong,
And lightsome as a locust-leaf,
Sir Launfal flashed forth in his maiden mail,
To seek in all climes for the Holy Grail.

### IV

It was morning on hill and stream and tree,
  And morning in the young knight's heart;
Only the castle moodily
Rebuffed the gifts of the sunshine free,
  And gloomed by itself apart;
The season brimmed all other things up
Full as the rain fills the pitcher-plant's cup.

### V

As Sir Launfal made morn through the darksome gate,
  He was 'ware of a leper, crouched by the same,
Who begged with his hand and moaned as he sate:
  And a loathing over Sir Launfal came;
The sunshine went out of his soul with a thrill,
  The flesh 'neath his armor 'gan to shrink and crawl,
And midway its leap his heart stood still
  Like a frozen waterfall;
For this man, so foul and bent of stature,
Rasped harshly against his dainty nature,
And seemed the one blot on the summer morn,—
So he tossed him a piece of gold in scorn.

## VI

The leper raised not the gold from the dust:
"Better to me the poor man's crust,
Better the blessing of the poor,
Though I turn me empty from his door;
That is no true alms which the hand can hold;
He gives only the worthless gold
    Who gives from a sense of duty;
But he who gives but a slender mite,
And gives to that which is out of sight,
    That thread of the all-sustaining Beauty
Which runs through all and doth all unite,—
The hand cannot clasp the whole of his alms,
The heart outstretches its eager palms,
For a god goes with it and makes it store
To the soul that was starving in darkness before."

### PRELUDE TO PART SECOND

Down swept the chill wind from the mountain peak,
    From the snow five thousand summers old;
On open wold and hill-top bleak
    It had gathered all the cold,
And whirled it like sleet on the wanderer's cheek;
It carried a shiver everywhere
From the unleafed boughs and pastures bare;
The little brook heard it and built a roof
'Neath which he could house him, winter-proof;
All night by the white stars' frosty gleams
He groined his arches and matched his beams;

216

Slender and clear were his crystal spars
As the lashes of light that trim the stars:
He sculptured every summer delight
In his halls and chambers out of sight;
Sometimes his tinkling waters slipt
Down through a frost-leaved forest-crypt,
Long, sparkling aisles of steel-stemmed trees
Bending to counterfeit a breeze;
Sometimes the roof no fretwork knew
But silvery mosses that downward grew;
Sometimes it was carved in sharp relief
With quaint arabesques of ice-fern leaf;
Sometimes it was simply smooth and clear
For the gladness of heaven to shine through, and here
He had caught the nodding bulrush-tops
And hung them thickly with diamond drops,
That crystalled the beams of moon and sun,
And made a star of every one:
No mortal builder's most rare device
Could match this winter-palace of ice;
'T was as if every image that mirrored lay
In his depths serene through the summer day,
Each fleeting shadow of earth and sky,
    Lest the happy model should be lost,
Had been mimicked in fairy masonry
    By the elfin builders of the frost.


Within the hall are song and laughter,
    The cheeks of Christmas glow red and jolly,
And sprouting is every corbel and rafter
    With lightsome green of ivy and holly;

Through the deep gulf of the chimney wide
Wallows the Yule-log's roaring tide;
The broad flame-pennons droop and flap
  And belly and tug as a flag in the wind;
Like a locust shrills the imprisoned sap,
  Hunted to death in its galleries blind;
And swift little troops of silent sparks,
  Now pausing, now scattering away as in fear,
Go threading the soot-forest's tangled darks
  Like herds of startled deer.

But the wind without was eager and sharp,
Of Sir Launfal's gray hair it makes a harp,
    And rattles and wrings
    The icy strings,
  Singing, in dreary monotone,
  A Christmas carol of its own,
  Whose burden still, as he might guess,
  Was—"Shelterless, shelterless, shelterless!"
The voice of the seneschal flared like a torch
As he shouted the wanderer away from the porch,
And he sat in the gateway and saw all night
  The great hall-fire, so cheery and bold,
  Through the window-slits of the castle old,
Build out its piers of ruddy light
Against the drift of the cold.

### PART SECOND

#### I

There was never a leaf on bush or tree,
The bare boughs rattled shudderingly;

The river was dumb and could not speak,
   For the weaver Winter its shroud had spun;
A single crow on the tree-top bleak
   From his shining feathers shed off the cold sun;
Again it was morning, but shrunk and cold,
As if her veins were sapless and old,
And she rose up decrepitly
For a last dim look at earth and sea.

## II

Sir Launfal turned from his own hard gate,
For another heir in his earldom sate;
An old, bent man, worn out and frail,
He came back from seeking the Holy Grail;
Little he recked of his earldom's loss,
No more on his surcoat was blazoned the cross,
But deep in his soul the sign he wore,
The badge of the suffering and the poor.

## III

Sir Launfal's raiment thin and spare
Was idle mail 'gainst the barbed air,
For it was just at the Christmas time;
So he mused, as he sat, of a sunnier clime,
And sought for a shelter from cold and snow
In the light and warmth of long-ago;
He sees the snake-like caravan crawl
O'er the edge of the desert, black and small,
Then nearer and nearer, till, one by one,
He can count the camels in the sun,

As over the red-hot sands they pass
To where, in its slender necklace of grass,
The little spring laughed and leapt in the shade,
And with its own self like an infant played,
And waved its signal of palms.

### IV

"For Christ's sweet sake, I beg an alms";—
The happy camels may reach the spring,
But Sir Launfal sees only the grewsome thing,
The leper, lank as the rain-blanched bone,
That cowers beside him, a thing as lone
And white as the ice-isles of Northern seas
In the desolate horror of his disease.

### V

And Sir Launfal said,—"I behold in thee
An image of Him who died on the tree;
Thou also hast had thy crown of thorns,—
Thou also hast had the world's buffets and scorns,—
And to thy life were not denied
The wounds in the hands and feet and side:
Mild Mary's Son, acknowledge me;
Behold, through him, I give to thee!"

### VI

Then the soul of the leper stood up in his eyes
    And looked at Sir Launfal, and straightway he
Remembered in what a haughtier guise
    He had flung an alms to leprosie,
When he girt his young life up in gilded mail
And set forth in search of the Holy Grail.

The heart within him was ashes and dust;
He parted in twain his single crust,
He broke the ice on the streamlet's brink
And gave the leper to eat and drink,
'T was a mouldy crust of coarse brown bread,
   'T was water out of a wooden bowl,—
Yet with fine wheaten bread was the leper fed,
    And 't was red wine he drank with his thirsty soul.

### VII

As Sir Launfal mused with a downcast face,
A light shone round about the place;
The leper no longer crouched at his side,
But stood before him glorified,
Shining and tall and fair and straight
As the pillar that stood by the Beautiful Gate,—
Himself the Gate whereby men can
Enter the temple of God in Man.

### VIII

His words were shed softer than leaves from the pine,
And they fell on Sir Launfal as snows on the brine,
That mingle their softness and quiet in one
With the shaggy unrest they float down upon;
And the voice that was softer than silence said,
"Lo it is I, be not afraid!
In many climes, without avail,
Thou has spent thy life for the Holy Grail;
Behold, it is here,—this cup which thou
Didst fill at the streamlet for me but now;
This crust is my body broken for thee,
This water his blood that died on the tree;

The Holy Supper is kept, indeed,
In whatso we share with another's need:
Not what we give, but what we share,
For the gift without the giver is bare;
Who gives himself with his alms feeds three,
Himself, his hungering neighbor, and me."

### IX

Sir Launfal awoke as from a swound:
"The Grail in my castle here is found!
Hang my idle armor up on the wall,
Let it be the spider's banquet-hall;
He must be fenced with stronger mail
Who would seek and find the Holy Grail."

### X

The castle gate stands open now,
    And the wanderer is welcome to the hall
As the hangbird is to the elm-tree bough;
    No longer scowl the turrets tall,
The Summer's long siege at last is o'er;
When the first poor outcast went in at the door,
She entered with him in disguise,
And mastered the fortress by surprise;
There is no spot she loves so well on ground,
She lingers and smiles there the whole year round;
The meanest serf on Sir Launfal's land
Has hall and bower at his command;
And there's no poor man in the North Countree
But is lord of the earldom as much as he.

*James Russell Lowell*

# Excelsior

The shades of night were falling fast,
As through an Alpine village passed
A youth, who bore, 'mid snow and ice,
A banner with the strange device,
                    Excelsior!

His brow was sad; his eye beneath,
Flashed like a falchion from its sheath,
And like a silver clarion rung
The accents of that unknown tongue,
                    Excelsior!

In happy homes he saw the light
Of household fires gleam warm and bright;
Above, the spectral glaciers shone,
And from his lips escaped a groan,
                    Excelsior!

"Try not to pass!" the old man said;
"Dark lowers the tempest overhead,
The roaring torrent is deep and wide!"
And loud that clarion voice replied,
                    Excelsior!

"Oh stay," the maiden said, "and rest
Thy weary head upon this breast!"
A tear stood in his bright blue eye,
But still he answered, with a sigh,
   Excelsior!

"Beware the pine-tree's withered branch!
Beware the awful avalanche!"
This was the peasant's last Good-night,
A voice replied, far up the height,
   Excelsior!

At break of day, as heavenward
The pious monks of Saint Bernard
Uttered the oft-repeated prayer,
A voice cried through the startled air,
   Excelsior!

A traveler, by the faithful hound,
Half buried in the snow was found,
Still grasping in his hand of ice
That banner with the strange device,
   Excelsior!

There in the twilight cold and gray,
Lifeless, but beautiful, he lay,
And from the sky, serene and far,
A voice fell, like a falling star,
   Excelsior!

*Henry Wadsworth Longfellow*

224

# The Fool's Prayer

The royal feast was done; the King
    Sought some new sport to banish care,
And to his jester cried: "Sir Fool,
    Kneel now, and make for us a prayer!"

The jester doffed his cap and bells,
    And stood the mocking court before;
They could not see the bitter smile
    Behind the painted grin he wore.

He bowed his head, and bent his knee
    Upon the monarch's silken stool;
His pleading voice arose: "O Lord,
    Be merciful to me, a fool!

"No pity, Lord, could change the heart
    From red with wrong to white as wool;
The rod must heal the sin: but Lord,
    Be merciful to me, a fool!

" 'Tis not by guilt the onward sweep
    Of truth and right, O Lord, we stay;
'Tis by our follies that so long
    We hold the earth from heaven away.

"These clumsy feet, still in the mire,
    Go crushing blossoms without end;
These hard, well-meaning hands we thrust
    Among the heart-strings of a friend.

"The ill-timed truth we might have kept—
    Who knows how sharp it pierced and stung?
The word we had not sense to say—
    Who knows how grandly it had rung!

"Our faults no tenderness should ask,
    The chastening stripes must cleanse them all;
But for our blunders—oh, in shame
    Before the eyes of heaven we fall.

"Earth bears no balsam for mistakes;
    Men crown the knave, and scourge the tool
That did his will; but Thou, O Lord,
    Be merciful to me, a fool!"

The room was hushed; in silence rose
    The King, and sought his gardens cool,
And walked apart, and murmured low,
    "Be merciful to me, a fool!"

                                *Edward  Rowland  Sill*

# He Fell Among Thieves

"Ye have robbed," said he, "ye have slaughtered and
    made an end,
  Take your ill-got plunder, and bury the dead:
What will ye more of your guest and sometime friend?"
  "Blood for our blood," they said.

He laughed: "If one may settle the score for five,
  I am ready; but let the reckoning stand till day:
I have loved the sunlight as dearly as any alive."
  "You shall die at dawn," said they.

He flung his empty revolver down the slope,
  He climbed alone to the Eastward edge of the trees;
All night long in a dream untroubled of hope
  He brooded, clasping his knees.

He did not hear the monotonous roar that fills
  The ravine where the Yassin river sullenly flows;
He did not see the starlight on the Laspur hills,
  Or the far Afghan snows.

He saw the April noon on his books aglow,
  The wistaria trailing in at the window wide;
He heard his father's voice from the terrace below
  Calling him down to ride.

He saw the gray little church across the park,
  The mounds that hid the loved and honored dead;
The Norman arch, the chancel softly dark,
  The brasses black and red.


He saw the School Close, sunny and green,
  The runner beside him, the stand by the parapet wall,
The distant tape, and the crowd roaring between,
  His own name over all.


He saw the dark wainscot and timbered roof,
  The long tables, and the faces merry and keen;
The College Eight, and their trainer dining aloof,
  The Dons on the dais serene.


He watched the liner's stem plowing the foam,
  He felt her trembling speed and the thrash of her
    screw;
He heard the passengers' voices talking of home,
  He saw the flag as she flew.


And now it was dawn. He rose strong on his feet,
  And strode to his ruined camp below the wood;
He drank the breath of the morning cool and sweet;
  His murderers round him stood.


Light on the Laspur hills was broadening fast,
  The blood-red snow-peaks chilled to a dazzling white;
He turned, and saw the golden circle at last,
  Cut by the Eastern height.

"O glorious Life, Who dwellest in earth and sun,
  I have lived, I praise and adore Thee."
                              A sword swept.
Over the pass the voices one by one
  Faded, and the hill slept.

*Henry Newbolt*

# Gunga Din

You may talk o' gin an' beer
When you're quartered safe out 'ere,
An' you're sent to penny-fights an' Aldershot it;
But when it comes to slaughter
You will do your work on water,
An' you'll lick the bloomin' boots of 'im that's got it.
Now in Injia's sunny clime,
Where I used to spend my time
A-servin' of 'Er Majesty the Queen,
Of all them black-faced crew
The finest man I knew
Was our regimental *bhisti,* Gunga Din.
    He was "Din! Din! Din!
    You limpin' lump o' brick-dust, Gunga Din!
    Hi! *slippey hitherao!*
    Water! get it! *Panee lao!*
    You squidgy-nosed old idol, Gunga Din!"

The uniform 'e wore
Was nothin' much before,
An' rather less than 'arf o' that be'ind,
For a piece o' twisty rag
An' a goatskin water-bag
Was all the field-equipment 'e could find.

When the sweatin' troop-train lay
In a sidin' through the day,
Where the 'eat would make your bloomin' eye-brows
      crawl,
We shouted *"Harry By!"*
Till our throats were bricky-dry,
Then we wopped 'im cause 'e couldn't serve us all.
      It was "Din! Din! Din!
      You 'eathen, where the mischief 'ave you been?
      You put some *juldee* in it
      Or I'll *marrow* you this minute
      If you don't fill up my helmet, Gunga Din!"


'E would dot an' carry one
Till the longest day was done;
An' 'e didn't seem to know the use o' fear.
If we charged or broke or cut,
You could bet your bloomin' nut,
'E'd be waitin' fifty paces right flank rear.
With 'is *mussick* on 'is back,
'E would skip with our attack,
An' watch us till the bugles made "Retire,"
An' for all 'is dirty 'ide
'E was white, clear white, inside
When 'e went to tend the wounded under fire!
      It was "Din! Din! Din!"
      With the bullets kickin' dust-spots on the green.
      When the cartridges ran out,
      You could 'ear the front-files shout,
      "Hi! ammunition-mules an' Gunga Din!"

I sha'n't forgit the night
When I dropped be'ind the fight
With a bullet where my belt-plate should 'a' been.
I was chokin' mad with thirst,
An' the man that spied me first
Was our good old grinnin', gruntin' Gunga Din.
'E lifted up my 'ead,
An' 'e plugged me where I bled,
An' 'e guv me 'arf-a-pint o' water—green:
It was crawlin' an' it stunk,
But of all the drinks I've drunk,
I'm gratefullest to one from Gunga Din.

      It was "Din! Din! Din!
      'Ere's a beggar with a bullet through 'is spleen;
      'E's chawin' up the ground,
      An' 'e's kickin' all around:
      For Gawd's sake git the water, Gunga Din!"

'E carried me away
To where a *dooli* lay,
An' a bullet come an' drilled the beggar clean.
'E put me safe inside,
An' just before 'e died:
"I 'ope you liked your drink," sez Gunga Din.
So I'll meet 'im later on
At the place where 'e is gone—
Where it's always double drill an' no canteen;
'E'll be squattin' on the coals,
Givin' drink to pore damned souls,
An' I'll git a swig in hell from Gunga Din!

Yes, Din! Din! Din!
You're a better man than I am, Gunga Din!
Though I've belted you an' flayed you,
By the livin' Gawd that made you,
You Lazarushian-leather Gunga Din!

*Rudyard Kipling*

# Cold Iron

*'Gold is for the mistress—silver for the maid—*
*Copper for the craftsman cunning at his trade.'*
'Good!' said the Baron, sitting in his hall,
'But Iron—Cold Iron—is master of them all.'

So he made rebellion 'gainst the King his liege,
Camped before his citadel and summoned it to siege.
'Nay!' said the cannoneer on the castle wall,
'But Iron—Cold Iron—shall be master of you all!'

Woe for the Baron and his knights so strong,
When the cruel cannon-balls laid 'em all along;
He was taken prisoner, he was cast in thrall,
And Iron—Cold Iron—was master of it all!

Yet his King spake kindly (ah, how kind a Lord!)
'What if I release thee now and give thee back thy sword?'
'Nay!' said the Baron, 'mock not at my fall,
For Iron—Cold Iron—is master of men all.'

*'Tears are for the craven, prayers are for the clown—*
*Halters for the silly neck that cannot keep a crown.'*
'As my loss is grievous, so my hope is small,
For Iron—Cold Iron—must be master of men all!'

Yet his King made answer (few such Kings there be!)
'Here is Bread and here is Wine—sit and sup with me.
Eat and drink in Mary's Name, the whiles I do recall
How Iron—Cold Iron—can be master of men all!'

He took the Wine and blessed it. He blessed and brake
    the Bread.
With His own Hands He served Them, and presently He
    said:
'See! These Hands they pierced with nails, outside My
    city wall,
Show Iron—Cold Iron—to be master of men all.

'Wounds are for the desperate, blows are for the strong.
Balm and oil for weary hearts all cut and bruised with
    wrong.
I forgive thy treason—I redeem thy fall—
For Iron—Cold Iron—must be master of men all!'

'*Crowns are for the valiant—sceptres for the bold!*
*Thrones and powers for mighty men who dare to take*
    *and hold!*'
'Nay!' said the Baron, kneeling in his hall,
'But Iron—Cold Iron—is master of men all!
Iron out of Calvary is master of men all!'

                                    *Rudyard Kipling*

235

# My True Love Hath My Heart

# Flowers in the Valley

O there was a woman, and she was a widow,
   Fair are the flowers in the valley.
With a daughter as fair as a fresh sunny meadow,
   The Red, the Green, and the Yellow,
The Harp, the Lute, the Pipe, the Flute, the Cymbal,
   Sweet goes the treble Violin.
The maid so rare and the flowers so fair
   Together they grew in the valley.


There came a Knight all clothed in red,
   Fair are the flowers in the valley.
'I would thou wert my bride,' he said,
   The Red, the Green, and the Yellow.
The Harp, the Lute, the Pipe, the Flute, the Cymbal,
   Sweet goes the treble Violin.
'I would,' she sighed, 'ne'er wins a bride!'
   Fair are the flowers in the valley.


There came a Knight all clothed in green,
   Fair are the flowers in the valley.
'This maid so sweet might be my queen.'
   The Red, the Green, and the Yellow.

The Harp, the Lute, the Pipe, the Flute, the Cymbal,
  Sweet goes the treble Violin.
'Might be,' sighed she, 'will ne'er win me!'
  Fair are the flowers in the valley.

There came a Knight, in yellow was he,
  Fair are the flowers in the valley,
'My bride, my queen, thou must with me!'
  The Red, the Green, and the Yellow.
The Harp, the Lute, the Pipe, the Flute, the Cymbal,
  Sweet goes the treble Violin.
With blushes red, 'I come,' she said;
  'Farewell to the flowers in the valley.'

*Traditional: English*

# Young Beichan and Susie Pye

In London was young Beichan born,
    He longed strange countries for to see;
But he was ta'en by a savage Moor,
    Who handled him right cruellie;

For he viewed the fashions of that land:
    Their way of worship viewèd he;
But to Mahound, or Termagant,
    Would Beichan never bend a knee.

So in every shoulder they've putten a bore,
    In every bore they've putten a tree,
And they have made him trail the wine
    And spices on his fair bodie.

They've casten him in a dungeon deep,
    Where he could neither hear nor see;
And fed him on naught but bread and water,
    Till he for hunger's like to dee.

This Moor he had but ae daughter,
    Her name was callèd Susie Pye;
And every day as she took the air,
    Near Beichan's prison she passed by.

And so it fell upon a day,
  About the middle time of Spring,
As she was passing by that way,
  She heard young Beichan sadly sing:


"My hounds they all run masterless,
  My hawks they fly frae tree to tree;
My youngest brother will heir my lands;
  Fair England again I'll never see.


"O were I free as I hae been,
  And my ship swimming once more on sea,
I'd turn my face to fair England,
  And sail no more to a strange countrie!"


All night long no rest she got,
  Young Beichan's song for thinking on;
She's stown the keys from her father's head,
  And to the prison strang is gone.


And she has opened the prison doors,
  I wot she opened two or three,
Ere she could come young Beichan at,
  He was locked up so curiouslie.


But when she cam' young Beichan till,
  Sore wondered he that may to see;
He took her for some fair captive:
  "Fair lady, I pray, of what countrie?"

"O have ye any lands," she said,
   "Or castles in your ain countrie,
That ye could give a lady fair,
   From prison strang to set you free?"


"Near London town I have a hall,
   And other castles two or three;
I'll give them all to the lady fair
   That out of prison will set me free."


"Give me the truth of your right hand,
   The truth of it give unto me,
That for seven years ye'll no lady wed,
   Unless it be alang wi' me."


"I'll give thee the truth of my right hand,
   The truth of it I'll freely gie,
That for seven years I'll stay unwed,
   For the kindness thou dost show to me."


And she has bribed the proud warder
   Wi' mickle gold and white monie;
She's gotten the keys of the prison strang,
   And she has set young Beichan free.


She's gi'en him to eat the good spice-cake;
   She's gi'en him to drink the blude-red wine;
She's bidden him sometimes think on her
   That sae kindly freed him out o' pine.

And she has broken her finger ring,
  And to Beichan half of it gave she;
"Keep it to mind you of that love
  The lady bore that set you free.


"And set your foot on good ship-board,
  And haste ye back to your ain countrie;
And before that seven years have an end,
  Come back again, love, and marry me."


But lang ere seven years had an end,
  She longed full sore her love to see;
So she's set her foot on good ship-board,
  And turned her back to her ain countrie.


She sailèd east, she sailèd west,
  Till to fair England's shore she came;
Where a bonny shepherd she espied,
  Feeding his sheep upon the plain.


"What news, what news, thou bonny shepherd?
  What news has thou to tell to me?"
"Such news I hear, ladie," he says,
  "The like was never in this countrie.


"There is a wedding in yonder hall,
  And ever the bells ring merrilie;
It is Lord Beichan's wedding-day
  Wi' a lady fair o' high degree."

She's putten her hand in her pocket,
   Gi'en him the gold and white monie;
"Here, take ye that, my bonny boy,
   All for the news thou tell'st to me."


When she came to young Beichan's gate,
   She tirlèd softly at the pin:
So ready was the proud porter
   To open and let this lady in.


"Is this young Beichan's hall," she said,
   "Or is that noble lord within?"
"Yea, he's in the hall among them all,
   And this is the day o' his weddin'."


"And has he wed anither love?
   And has he clean forgotten me?"
And, sighin', said that ladie gay,
   "I wish I were in my ain countrie."


And she has ta'en her gay gold ring,
   That with her love she brake sae free;
Says, "Gie him that, ye proud porter,
   And bid the bridegroom speak wi' me."


When the porter came his lord before,
   He kneelèd low upon his knee—
"What aileth thee, my proud porter,
   Thou art so full of courtesie?"

"I've been porter at your gates,
    It's now for thirty years and three;
But there stands a lady at them now,
    The like o' her did I never see;


"For on every finger she has a ring,
    And on her mid-finger she has three;
And meikle gold aboon her brow.
    Sae fair a may did I never see."


It's out then spak the bride's mother,
    Aye and an angry woman was she:
"Ye might have excepted our bonny bride,
    And twa or three of our companie."


"O haud your tongue, thou bride's mother,
    Of all your folly let me be;
She's ten times fairer nor the bride,
    And all that's in your companie.


"And this golden ring that's broken in twa,
    This half o' a golden ring sends she:
'Ye'll carry that to Lord Beichan,' she says,
    'And bid him come an' spak wi' me.'


"She begs one sheave of your white bread,
    But and a cup of your red wine;
And to remember the lady's love,
    That last relieved you out of pine."

245

"O well-a-day!" said Beichan then,
   "That I so soon have married me!
For it can be none but Susie Pye,
   That for my love has sailed the sea."


And quickly hied he down the stair;
   Of fifteen steps he made but three;
He's ta'en his bonny love in his arms,
   And kist, and kist her tenderlie.


"O hae ye ta'en anither bride?
   And hae ye quite forgotten me?
And hae ye quite forgotten her,
   That gave you life and libertie?"


She lookit o'er her left shoulder,
   To hide the tears stood in her e'e;
"Now fare thee well, young Beichan," she says,
   "I'll try to think no more on thee."


"O never, never, Susie Pye,
   For surely this can never be;
Nor ever shall I wed but her
   That's done and dreed so much for me."


Then out and spak the forenoon bride:
   "My lord, your love it changeth soon;
This morning I was made your bride,
   And another's chose ere it be noon."

"O haud thy tongue, thou forenoon bride:
  Ye're ne'er a whit the worse for me;
And whan ye return to your own land,
  A double dower I'll send wi' thee."

He's ta'en Susie Pye by the white hand,
  And gently led her up and down;
And ay, as he kist her red rosy lips,
  "Ye're welcome, jewel, to your own."

He's ta'en her by her milk-white hand,
  And led her to yon fountain stane;
He's changed her name from Susie Pye,
  And called her his bonny love, Lady Jane.

*Traditional: English*

# Alice Brand

Merry it is in the good greenwood,
  When the mavis and merle are singing,
When the deer sweeps by, and the hounds are in cry,
  And the hunter's horn is ringing.

"O Alice Brand, my native land
  Is lost for love of you;
And we must hold by wood and wold,
  As outlaws wont to do.

"O Alice, 'twas all for thy locks so bright,
  And 'twas all for thine eyes so blue,
That on the night of our luckless flight,
  Thy brother bold I slew.

"Now must I teach to hew the beech
  The hand that held the glaive,
For leaves to spread our lowly bed,
  And stakes to fence our cave.

"And for vest of pall, thy fingers small,
  They wont on harp to stray,
A cloak must shear from the slaughtered deer,
  To keep the cold away."

"O Richard! if my brother died,
  'Twas but a fatal chance;
For darkling was the battle tried,
  And fortune sped the lance.

"If pall and vair no more I wear,
  Nor thou the crimson sheen,
As warm, we'll say, is the russet gray,
  As gay the forest green.

"And, Richard, if our lot be hard,
  And lost thy native land,
Still Alice has her own Richard,
  And he his Alice Brand."

## II

'Tis merry, 'tis merry, in good greenwood,
  So blithe Lady Alice is singing;
On the beech's pride, and oak's brown side,
  Lord Richard's ax is ringing.

Up spoke the moody Elfin King,
  Who woned within the hill,—
Like wind in the porch of a ruined church,
  His voice was ghostly shrill.

"Why sounds yon stroke on beech and oak,
  Our moonlight circle's screen?
Or who comes here to chase the deer,
  Beloved of our Elfin Queen?
Or who may dare on wold to wear
  The fairies' fatal green?

"Up, Urgan, up! to yon mortal hie,
  For thou wert christened man;
For cross or sign thou wilt not fly,
  For muttered word or ban.

"Lay on him the curse of the withered heart,
  The curse of the sleepless eye;
Till he wish and pray that his life would part,
  Nor yet find leave to die!"

### III

'Tis merry, 'tis merry, in good greenwood,
  Though the birds have stilled their singing;
The evening blaze doth Alice raise,
  And Richard is fagots bringing.

Up Urgan starts, that hideous dwarf,
  Before Lord Richard stands,
And, as he crossed and blessed himself,
"I fear not sign," quoth the grisly elf,
  "That is made with bloody hands."

But out then spoke she, Alice Brand,
  That woman void of fear,—
"And if there's blood upon his hand,
  'Tis but the blood of deer."

"Now loud thou liest, thou bold of mood!
  It cleaves unto his hand,
The stain of thine own kindly blood,
  The blood of Ethert Brand."

Then forward stepped she, Alice Brand,
 And made the holy sign,—
"And if there's blood on Richard's hand,
 A spotless hand is mine.

"And I conjure thee, Demon elf,
 By Him whom Demons fear,
To show us whence thou art thyself,
 And what thine errand here?"

### IV

" 'Tis merry, 'tis merry, in Fairy-land,
 When fairy birds are singing,
When the court doth ride by the monarch's side,
 With bit and bridle ringing.

"And gaily shines the Fairy-land—
 But all is glistening show,
Like the idle gleam that December's beam
 Can dart on ice and snow.

"And fading, like that varied gleam,
 Is our inconstant shape,
Who now like knight and lady seem,
 And now like dwarf and ape.

"It was between the night and day,
 When the Fairy King has power,
That I sunk down in a sinful fray,
And, 'twixt life and death, was snatched away
 To the joyless Elfin bower.

"But wist I of a woman bold,
    Who thrice my brow durst sign,
I might regain my mortal mold,
    As fair a form as thine."

She crossed him once—she crossed him twice—
    That lady was so brave;
The fouler grew his goblin hue,
    The darker grew the cave.

She crossed him thrice, that lady bold;
    He rose beneath her hand
The fairest knight on Scottish mold,
    Her brother, Ethert Brand!

Merry it is in good greenwood,
    When the mavis and merle are singing,
But merrier were they in Dunfermline grey,
    When all the bells were ringing.

*Walter Scott*

# Lady Clare

It was the time when lilies blow,
　　And clouds are highest up in air,
Lord Ronald brought a lily-white doe
　　To give his cousin, Lady Clare.

I trow they did not part in scorn:
　　Lovers long-betrothed were they:
They two will wed the morrow morn,—
　　God's blessing on the day!

"He does not love me for my birth,
　　Nor for my lands so broad and fair;
He loves me for my own true worth,
　　And that is well," said Lady Clare.

In there came old Alice the nurse,
　　Said, "Who was this that went from thee?"
"It was my cousin," said Lady Clare,
　　"To-morrow he weds with me."

"O God be thanked!" said Alice the nurse,
　　"That all comes round so just and fair:
Lord Ronald is heir of all your lands,
　　And you are *not* the Lady Clare."

"Are ye out of your mind, my nurse, my nurse,"
    Said Lady Clare, "that ye speak so wild?"
"As God's above," said Alice the nurse,
    "I speak the truth: you are my child.

"The old earl's daughter died at my breast;
    I speak the truth, as I live by bread!
I buried her like my own sweet child,
    And put my child in her stead."

"Falsely, falsely have ye done,
    O mother," she said, "if this be true,
To keep the best man under the sun
    So many years from his due."

"Nay now, my child," said Alice the nurse,
    "But keep the secret for your life,
And all you have will be Lord Ronald's,
    When you are man and wife."

"If I'm a beggar born," she said,
    "I will speak out, for I dare not lie.
Pull off, pull off, the brooch of gold,
    And fling the diamond necklace by."

"Nay now, my child," said Alice the nurse,
    "But keep the secret all you can."
She said, "Not so: but I will know
    If there be faith in man."

"Nay now, what faith?" said Alice the nurse,
  "The man will cleave unto his right."
"And he shall have it," the lady replied,
  "Though I should die to-night."


"Yet give one kiss to your mother dear,
  Alas, my child, I sinned for thee."
"O mother, mother, mother," she said,
  "So strange it seems to me.


"Yet here's a kiss for my mother dear,
  My mother dear, if this be so,
And lay your hand upon my head,
  And bless me, mother, ere I go."


She clad herself in a russet gown,
  She was no longer Lady Clare:
She went by dale, and she went by down,
  With a single rose in her hair.


The lily-white doe Lord Ronald had brought
  Leaped up from where she lay,
Dropped her head in the maiden's hand,
  And followed her all the way.


Down stepped Lord Ronald from his tower:
  "O Lady Clare, you shame your worth!
Why come you dressed like a village maid,
  That are the flower of the earth?"

"If I come dressed like a village maid,
　I am but as my fortunes are:
I am a beggar born," she said,
　"And not the Lady Clare."

"Play me no tricks," said Lord Ronald,
　"For I am yours in word and in deed.
Play me no tricks," said Lord Ronald,
　"Your riddle is hard to read."

O, and proudly stood she up!
　Her heart within her did not fail;
She looked into Lord Ronald's eyes,
　And told him all her nurse's tale.

He laughed a laugh of merry scorn:
　He turned and kissed her where she stood:
"If you are not the heiress born,
　And I," said he, "the next in blood—

"If you are not the heiress born,
　And I," said he, "the lawful heir,
We two will wed to-morrow morn,
　And you shall still be Lady Clare."

*Alfred Tennyson*

# The Beggar Maid

Her arms across her breast she laid;
   She was more fair than words can say:
Bare-footed came the beggar maid
   Before the king Cophetua.
In robe and crown the king stepped down,
   To meet and greet her on her way;
"It is no wonder," said the lords,
   "She is more beautiful than day."

As shines the moon in clouded skies,
   She in her poor attire was seen:
One praised her ankles, one her eyes,
   One her dark hair and lovesome mien.
So sweet a face, such angel grace,
   In all that land had never been:
Cophetua sware a royal oath:
   "This beggar maid shall be my queen!"

*Alfred Tennyson*

# Annabel Lee

It was many and many a year ago,
   In a kingdom by the sea,
That a maiden there lived whom you may know
   By the name of Annabel Lee;
And this maiden she lived with no other thought
   Than to love and be loved by me.

I was a child and she was a child,
   In this kingdom by the sea,
But we loved with a love that was more than love,
   I and my Annabel Lee;
With a love that the winged seraphs of heaven
   Coveted her and me.

And this was the reason that, long ago,
   In this kingdom by the sea,
A wind blew out of a cloud, chilling
   My beautiful Annabel Lee;
So that her highborn kinsmen came
   And bore her away from me,
To shut her up in a sepulcher
   In this kingdom by the sea.

The angels, not half so happy in heaven,
    Went envying her and me;
Yes! that was the reason (as all men know,
    In this kingdom by the sea)
That the wind came out of the cloud by night,
    Chilling and killing my Annabel Lee.

But our love it was stronger by far than the love
    Of those who were older than we,
    Of many far wiser than we;
And neither the angels in heaven above,
    Nor the demons down under the sea,
Can ever dissever my soul from the soul
    Of the beautiful Annabel Lee:

For the moon never beams, without bringing me dreams
    Of the beautiful Annabel Lee;
And the stars never rise, but I feel the bright eyes
    Of the beautiful Annabel Lee;
And so, all the night-tide, I lie down by the side
Of my darling—my darling—my life and my bride,
    In the sepulcher there by the sea,
    In her tomb by the sounding sea.

*Edgar Allan Poe*

# The Cap and Bells

The jester walked in the garden:
The garden had fallen still;
He bade his soul rise upward
And stand on her window-sill.

It rose in a straight blue garment,
When owls began to call:
It had grown wise-tongued by thinking
Of a quiet and light footfall;

But the young queen would not listen;
She rose in her pale night-gown;
She drew in the heavy casement
And pushed the latches down.

He bade his heart go to her,
When the owls called out no more;
In a red and quivering garment
It sang to her through the door.

It had grown sweet-tongued by dreaming
Of a flutter of flower-like hair;
And she took up her fan from the table
And waved it off on the air.

'I have cap and bells,' he pondered,
'I will send them to her and die';
And when the morning whitened
He left them where she went by.

She laid them upon her bosom,
Under a cloud of her hair,
And her red lips sang them a love-song
Till stars grew out of the air.

She opened her door and her window,
And the heart and the soul came through,
To her right hand came the red one,
To her left hand came the blue.

They set up a noise like crickets,
A chattering wise and sweet,
And her hair was a folded flower
And the quiet of love in her feet.

*William Butler Yeats*

# Patterns

I walk down the garden paths,
And all the daffodils
Are blowing, and the bright blue squills.
I walk down the patterned garden-paths
In my stiff, brocaded gown.
With my powdered hair and jewelled fan,
I too am a rare
Pattern. As I wander down
The garden paths.

My dress is richly figured,
And the train
Makes a pink and silver stain
On the gravel, and the thrift
Of the borders.
Just a plate of current fashion,
Tripping by in high-heeled, ribboned shoes.
Not a softness anywhere about me,
Only whale-bone and brocade.
And I sink on a seat in the shade
Of a lime-tree. For my passion
Wars against the stiff brocade.
The daffodils and squills
Flutter in the breeze

As they please.
And I weep;
For the lime-tree is in blossom
And one small flower has dropped upon my bosom.

And the plashing of waterdrops
In the marble fountain
Comes down the garden-paths.
The dripping never stops.
Underneath my stiffened gown
Is the softness of a woman bathing in a marble basin,
A basin in the midst of hedges grown
So thick, she cannot see her lover hiding.
But she guesses he is near,
And the sliding of the water
Seems the stroking of a dear
Hand upon her.
What is Summer in a fine brocaded gown!
I should like to see it lying in a heap upon the ground.
All the pink and silver crumpled upon the ground.

I would be the pink and silver as I ran along the paths,
And he would stumble after,
Bewildered by my laughter.
I should see the sun flashing from his sword-hilt and the
        buckles on his shoes.
I would choose
To lead him in a maze along the patterned paths,
A bright and laughing maze for my heavy-booted lover,
Till he caught me in the shade,
And the buttons of his waistcoat bruised my body as he
        clasped me,

Aching, melting, unafraid.
With the shadows of the leaves and the sundrops,
And the plopping of the waterdrops,
All about us in the open afternoon—
I am very like to swoon
With the weight of this brocade,
For the sun sifts through the shade.


Underneath the fallen blossom
In my bosom,
Is a letter I have hid.
It was brought to me this morning by a rider from the
        Duke.
"Madam, we regret to inform you that Lord Hartwell
Died in action Thursday se'nnight."
As I read it in the white, morning sunlight,
The letters squirmed like snakes.
"Any answer, Madam?" said my footman.
"No," I told him.
"See that the messenger takes some refreshment.
No, no answer."
And I walked into the garden,
Up and down the patterned paths,
In my stiff, correct brocade.
The blue and yellow flowers stood up proudly in the sun,
Each one.
I stood upright too,
Held rigid to the pattern
By the stiffness of my gown.
Up and down I walked,
Up and down.

In a month he would have been my husband.
In a month, here, underneath this lime,
He would have broke the pattern;
He for me, and I for him,
He as Colonel, I as Lady,
On this shady seat.
He had a whim
That sunlight carried blessing.
And I answered, "It shall be as you have said."
Now he is dead.

In Summer and in Winter I shall walk
Up and down
The patterned garden-paths
In my stiff, brocaded gown.
The squills and daffodils
Will give place to pillared roses, and to asters, and to
        snow.
I shall go
Up and down,
In my gown.
Gorgeously arrayed,
Boned and stayed.
And the softness of my body will be guarded from em-
        brace
By each button, hook and lace.
For the man who should loose me is dead,
Fighting with the Duke of Flanders,
In a pattern called a war.
Christ! What are patterns for?

                                        *Amy Lowell*

# Fantasy and Enchantment

# The Wind and the Moon

Said the Wind to the Moon, "I will blow you out;
> You stare
> In the air
> Like a ghost in a chair,
Always looking what I am about—
I hate to be watched; I'll blow you out."

The Wind blew hard, and out went the Moon.
> So, deep
> On a heap
> Of clouds to sleep,
Down lay the Wind, and slumbered soon,
Muttering low, "I've done for that Moon."

He turned in his bed; she was there again!
> On high
> In the sky,
> With her one ghost eye,
The Moon shone white and alive and plain.
Said the Wind, "I will blow you out again."

The Wind blew hard, and the Moon grew dim.
> "With my sledge,
> And my wedge,
> I have knocked off her edge!

If only I blow right fierce and grim,
The creature will soon be dimmer than dim."


He blew and he blew, and she thinned to a thread.
        "One puff
        More's enough
        To blow her to snuff!
One good puff more where the last was bred,
And glimmer, glimmer, glum will go the thread."


He blew a great blast, and the thread was gone.
        In the air
        Nowhere
        Was a moonbeam bare;
Far off and harmless the shy stars shone—
Sure and certain the Moon was gone!


The Wind he took to his revels once more;
        On down,
        In town,
        Like a merry-mad clown,
He leaped and halloed with whistle and roar—
"What's that?" The glimmering thread once more!


He flew in a rage—he danced and blew;
        But in vain
        Was the pain
        Of his bursting brain;
For still the broader the Moon-scrap grew,
The broader he swelled his big cheeks and blew.

Slowly she grew—till she filled the night,
>> And shone
>> On her throne
>> In the sky alone,
A matchless, wonderful silvery light,
Radiant and lovely, the queen of the night.

Said the Wind: "What a marvel of power am I!
>> With my breath,
>> Good faith!
>> I blew her to death—
First blew her away right out of the sky—
Then blew her in; what strength have I!"

But the Moon she knew nothing about the affair;
>> For high
>> In the sky
>> With her one white eye,
Motionless, miles above the air,
She had never heard the great Wind blare.

*George Macdonald*

# The Fairy Thorn

"Get up, our Anna dear, from the weary spinning wheel;
   For your father's on the hill, and your mother is asleep:
Come up above the crags, and we'll dance a highland reel
    Around the fairy thorn on the steep."


At Anna Grace's door 'twas thus the maidens cried,
   Three merry maidens fair in kirtles of the green;
And Anna laid the rock and the weary wheel aside,
    The fairest of the four, I ween.


They're glancing through the glimmer of the quiet eve,
   Away in milky wavings of neck and ankle bare;
The heavy-sliding stream in its sleep song they leave,
    And the crags in the ghostly air.


And linking hand in hand, and singing as they go,
    The maids along the hill-side have ta'en their fearless
      way,
Till they come to where the rowan trees in lonely beauty
      grow
    Beside the Fairy Hawthorn grey.

The hawthorn stands between the ashes tall and slim,
  Like matron with her twin grand-daughters at her knee;
The rowan berries cluster o'er her low head grey and dim
    In ruddy kisses sweet to see.

The merry maidens four have ranged them in a row,
  Between each lovely couple a stately rowan stem,
And away in mazes wavy, like skimming birds they go,
    Oh, never carolled bird like them!

But solemn is the silence of the silvery haze
  That drinks away their voices in echoless repose,
And dreamily the evening has stilled the haunted braes,
    And dreamier the gloaming grows.

And sinking one by one, like lark-notes from the sky
  When the falcon's shadow saileth across the open shaw,
Are hushed the maidens' voices, as cowering down they lie
    In the flutter of their sudden awe.

For, from the air above, and the grassy ground beneath,
  And from the mountain-ashes and the old whitethorn
    between,
A power of faint enchantment doth through their beings
    breathe,
    And they sink down together on the green.

They sink together silent, and stealing side to side,
  They fling their lovely arms o'er their drooping necks
    so fair.

Then vainly strive again their naked arms to hide,
   For their shrinking necks again are bare.


Thus clasped and prostrate all, with their heads together
      bowed,
   Soft o'er their bosoms' beating—the only human
      sound—
They hear the silky footsteps of the silent fairy crowd,
   Like a river in the air, gliding round.


Nor scream can any raise, nor prayer can any say,
   But wild, wild, the terror of the speechless three—
For they feel fair Anna Grace drawn silently away,
   By whom they dare not look to see.


They feel their tresses twine with her parting locks of
      gold,
   And the curls elastic falling, as her head withdraws;
They feel her sliding arms from their trancèd arms un-
      fold,
   But they dare not look to see the cause:


For heavy on their senses the faint enchantment lies
   Through all that night of anguish and perilous amaze;
And neither fear nor wonder can ope their quivering eyes
   Or their limbs from the cold ground raise,


Till out of Night the Earth has rolled her dewy side,
   With every haunted mountain and streamy vale below;
When, as the mist dissolves in the yellow morning-tide,
   The maidens' trance dissolveth so.

Then fly the ghastly three as swiftly as they may,
    And tell their tale of sorrow to anxious friends in
       vain—
They pined away and died within the year and day,
    And ne'er was Anna Grace seen again.

*Samuel Ferguson*

# Thomas the Rhymer

True Thomas lay on Huntlie bank;
  A ferlie he spied wi' his e'e;
And there he saw a lady bright,
  Come riding down by the Eildon Tree.

Her skirt was o' the grass-green silk,
  Her mantle o' the velvet fine;
At ilka tett o' her horse's mane
  Hung fifty siller bells and nine.

True Thomas he pu'd aff his cap,
  And louted low down on his knee:
"Hail to thee, Mary, Queen of Heaven!
  For thy peer on earth could never be."

"O no, O no, Thomas!" she said,
  "That name does not belang to me;
I'm but the Queen o' fair Elfland,
  That am hither come to visit thee.

"Harp and carp, Thomas!" she said,
  "Harp and carp along wi' me;
And if ye dare to kiss my lips,
  Sure of your body I will be."

"Betide me weal, betide me woe,
    That weird shall never daunten me."
Syne he has kissed her rosy lips,
    All underneath the Eildon Tree.


"Now, ye maun go wi' me," she said;
    "True Thomas, ye maun go wi' me;
And ye maun serve me seven years,
    Through weal or woe as may chance to be."


She's mounted on her milk-white steed;
    She's ta'en true Thomas up behind;
And aye, whene'er her bridle rang,
    The steed gaed swifter than the wind.


O they rade on, and father on,
    The steed gaed swifter than the wind;
Until they reached a desert wide,
    And living land was left behind.


"Light down, light down now, true Thomas,
    And lean your head upon my knee;
Abide ye there a little space,
    And I will show you ferlies three.


"O see ye not yon narrow road,
    So thick beset wi' thorns and briers?
That is the Path of Righteousness,
    Though after it but few inquires.

"And see ye not yon braid, braid road,
  That lies across the lily leven?
That is the Path of Wickedness,
  Though some call it the Road to Heaven.


"And see ye not yon bonny road
  That winds about the fernie brae?
That is the Road to fair Elfland,
  Where thou and I this night maun gae.


"But, Thomas, ye sall haud your tongue,
  Whatever ye may hear or see;
For speak ye word in Elfyn-land,
  Ye'll ne'er win back to your ain countrie."


O they rade on, and farther on,
  And they waded rivers abune the knee;
And they saw neither sun nor moon,
  But they heard the roaring of the sea.


It was mirk, mirk night, there was nae starlight,
  They waded through red blude to the knee;
For a' the blude that's shed on earth
  Rins through the springs o' that countrie.


Syne they came to a garden green,
  And she pu'd an apple frae a tree:
"Take this for thy wages, true Thomas;
  It will give thee tongue that can never lee."

"My tongue is mine ain," true Thomas he said;
  "A gudely gift ye wad gie to me!
I neither dought to buy nor sell,
  At fair or tryst where I might be.

"I dought neither speak to prince or peer,
  Nor ask of grace from fair lady!"
"Now haud thy peace!" the lady said,
  "For as I say, so must it be."

He has gotten a coat of the even cloth,
  And a pair o' shoon of the velvet green;
And till seven years were gane and past,
  True Thomas on earth was never seen.

*Traditional: Scots*

# The Fairies

Up the airy mountain,
   Down the rushy glen,
We daren't go a-hunting
   For fear of little men;
Wee folk, good folk,
   Trooping all together;
Green jacket, red cap,
   And white's owl's feather!

Down along the rocky shore
   Some make their home,
They live on crispy pancakes
   Of yellow-tide foam;
Some in the reeds
   Of the black mountain lake,
With frogs for their watch-dogs,
   All night awake.

High on the hill-top
   The old King sits;
He is now so old and gray
   He's nigh lost his wits.

With a bridge of white mist
  Columbkill he crosses,
On his stately journeys
  From Slieveleague to Rosses;
Or going up with music
  On cold starry nights
To sup with the Queen
Of the gay Northern Lights.


They stole little Bridget
  For seven years long;
When she came down again
  Her friends were all gone.
They took her lightly back,
  Between the night and morrow,
They thought that she was fast asleep.
  But she was dead with sorrow.
They have kept her ever since
  Deep within the lake,
On a bed of flag-leaves,
  Watching till she wake.


By the craggy hill-side,
  Through the mosses bare,
They have planted thorn-trees
  For pleasure here and there.
If any man so daring
  As dig them up in spite,
He shall find their sharpest thorns
  In his bed at night.

### THE FAIRIES

Up the airy mountain,
  Down the rushy glen,
We daren't go a-hunting
  For fear of little men;
Wee folk, good folk,
  Trooping all together;
Green jacket, red cap,
  And white owl's feather!

*William  Allingham*

# The Seven Fiddlers

A blue robe on their shoulders,
   And an ivory bow in hand,
Seven fiddlers came with their fiddles
   A-fiddling through the land,
And they fiddled a tune on their fiddles
   That none could understand.

For none who heard their fiddling
   Might keep his ten toes still,
E'en the cripple threw down his crutches,
   And danced against his will:
Young and old they fell a-dancing,
   While the fiddlers fiddle their fill.

They fiddled down to the ferry—
   The ferry by Severn-side,
And they stept aboard the ferry,
   None else to row or guide,
And deftly steered the pilot,
   And stoutly the oars they plied.

Then suddenly in mid-channel
   These fiddlers ceased to row,
And the pilot spake to his fellows
   In a tongue that none may know:

"Let us home to our fathers and brothers,
  And the maidens we love below."

Then the fiddlers seized their fiddles,
  And sang to their fiddles a song:
"We are coming, coming, oh brothers,
  To the home we have left so long,
For the world still loves the fiddler,
  And the fiddler's tune is strong."

Then they stepped from out the ferry
  Into the Severn-sea,
Down into the depths of the waters
  Where the homes of the fiddlers be,
And the ferry-boat drifted slowly
  Forth to the ocean free!

But where those jolly fiddlers
  Walked down into the deep,
The ripples are never quiet,
  But forever dance and leap,
Though the Severn-sea be silent,
  And the winds be all asleep.

*Sebastian Evans*

# A Musical Instrument

What was he doing, the great god Pan,
    Down in the reeds by the river?
Spreading ruin and scattering ban,
Splashing and paddling with hoofs of a goat,
And breaking the golden lilies afloat
    With the dragon-fly on the river.

He tore out a reed, the great god Pan,
    From the deep cool bed of the river:
The limpid water turbidly ran,
And the broken lilies a-dying lay,
And the dragon-fly had fled away,
    Ere he brought it out of the river.

High on the shore sat the great god Pan,
    While turbidly flowed the river;
And hacked and hewed as a great god can,
With his hard bleak steel at the patient reed,
Till there was not a sign of a leaf indeed
    To prove it fresh from the river.

He cut it short, did the great god Pan,
    (How tall it stood in the river!)
Then drew the pith, like the heart of a man,
Steadily from the outside ring,

And notched the poor dry empty thing
   In holes, as he sat by the river.

"This is the way," laughed the great god Pan,
   (Laughed while he sat by the river,)
"The only way, since gods began
To make sweet music, they could succeed."
Then, dropping his mouth to a hole in the reed,
   He blew in power by the river.

Sweet, sweet, sweet, O Pan!
   Piercing sweet by the river!
Blinding sweet, O great god Pan!
The sun on the hill forgot to die,
And the lilies revived, and the dragon-fly
   Came back to dream on the river.

Yet half a beast is the great god Pan,
   To laugh as he sits by the river,
Making a poet out of a man:
The true gods sigh for the cost and pain,—
For the reed which grows nevermore again
   As a reed with the reeds in the river.

*Elizabeth Barrett Browning*

# Eve

Eve, with her basket, was
Deep in the bells and grass,
Wading in bells and grass
Up to her knees,
Picking a dish of sweet
Berries and plums to eat,
Down in the bells and grass
Under the trees.

Mute as a mouse in a
Corner the cobra lay,
Curled round a bough of the
Cinnamon tall. . . .
Now to get even and
Humble proud heaven and
Now was the moment or
Never at all.

"Eva!" Each syllable
Light as a flower fell,
"Eva!" he whispered the
Wondering maid,

Soft as a bubble sung
Out of a linnet's lung,
Soft and most silverly
"Eva!" he said.

Picture that orchard sprite,
Eve, with her body white,
Supple and smooth to her
Slim finger tips,
Wondering, listening,
Listening, wondering,
Eve with a berry
Half-way to her lips.

Oh, had our simple Eve
Seen through the make-believe!
Had she but known the
Pretender he was!
Out of the boughs he came,
Whispering still her name,
Tumbling in twenty rings
Into the grass.

Here was the strangest pair
In the world anywhere,
Eve in the bells and grass
Kneeling, and he
Telling his story low. . . .
Singing birds saw them go
Down the dark path to
The Blasphemous Tree.

Oh, what a clatter when
Titmouse and Jenny Wren
Saw him successful and
Taking his leave!
How the birds rated him,
How they all hated him!
How they all pitied
Poor motherless Eve!

Picture her crying
Outside in the lane,
Eve, with no dish of sweet
Berries and plums to eat,
Haunting the gate of the
Orchard in vain. . . .
Picture the lewd delight
Under the hill to-night—
"Eva!" the toast goes round,
"Eva!" again.

*Ralph Hodgson*

# The Dancing Seal

When we were building Skua Light—
The first men who had lived a night
Upon that deep-sea Isle—
As soon as chisel touched the stone,
The friendly seals would come ashore;
And sit and watch us all the while,
As though they'd not seen men before;
And so, poor beasts, had never known
Men had the heart to do them harm.
They'd little cause to feel alarm
With us, for we were glad to find
Some friendliness in that strange sea;
Only too pleased to let them be
And sit as long as they'd a mind
To watch us: for their eyes were kind
Like women's eyes, it seemed to me.
So, hour on hour, they sat: I think
They liked to hear the chisels' clink:
And when the boy sang loud and clear,
They scrambled closer in to hear;
And if he whistled sweet and shrill,
The queer beasts shuffled nearer still:
But every sleek and sheeny skin
Was mad to hear his violin.

When, work all over for the day,
He'd take his fiddle down and play
His merry tunes beside the sea
Their eyes grew brighter and more bright
And burned and twinkled merrily:
And as I watched them one still night,
And saw their eager sparkling eyes,
I felt those lively seals would rise
Some shiny night ere he could know,
And dance about him, heel and toe,
Unto the fiddle's heady tune.

And at the rising of the moon,
Half-daft, I took my stand before
A young seal lying on the shore;
And called on her to dance with me.
And it seemed hardly strange when she
Stood up before me suddenly,
And shed her black and sheeny skin;
And smiled, all eager to begin  . . .
And I was dancing, heel and toe,
With a young maiden white as snow,
Unto a crazy violin.

We danced beneath the dancing moon
All night, beside the dancing sea,
With tripping toes and skipping heels:
And all about us friendly seals
Like Christian folk were dancing reels
Unto the fiddle's endless tune
That kept on spinning merrily
As though it never meant to stop.

And never once the snow-white maid
A moment stayed
To take a breath,
Though I was fit to drop:
And while those wild eyes challenged me,
I knew as well as well could be
I must keep step with that young girl,
Though we should dance to death.

'Then with a skirl
The fiddle broke:
The moon went out:
The sea stopped dead:
And, in a twinkling, all the rout
Of dancing folk had fled . . .
And in the chill bleak dawn I woke
Upon the naked rock, alone.

They've brought me far from Skua Isle . . .
I laugh to think they do not know
That as, all day, I chip the stone,
Among my fellows here inland,
I smell the sea-wrack on the shore . . .
And see her snowy-tossing hand,
And meet again her merry smile . . .
And dream I'm dancing all the while
I'm dancing ever, heel and toe,
With a seal-maiden, white as snow,
On that moonshiny, Island-strand,
For ever and for evermore.

*Wilfrid Gibson*

# Sam

When Sam goes back in memory,
   It is to where the sea
Breaks on the shingle, emerald-green
   In white foam, endlessly;
He says—with small brown eye on mine—
   'I used to keep awake,
And lean from my window in the moon,
   Watching those billows break.
And half a million tiny hands,
   And eyes, like sparks of frost,
Would dance and come tumbling into the moon,
   On every breaker tossed.
And all across from star to star,
   I've seen the watery sea,
With not a single ship in sight,
   Just ocean there, and me;
And heard my father snore . . . And once,
   As sure as I'm alive,
Out of those wallowing, moon-flecked waves
   I saw a mermaid dive;
Head and shoulders above the wave,
   Plain as I now see you,
Combing her hair, now back, now front,
   Her two eyes peeping through;

Calling me, "Sam!"—quietlike—"Sam!" . . .
  But me . . . I never went,
Making believe I kind of thought
  'Twas someone else she meant . . .
Wonderful lovely there she sat,
  Singing the night away,
All in the solitudinous sea
  Of that there lonely bay.
P'raps,' and he'd smooth his hairless mouth,
  'P'raps, if 'twere *now*, my son,
P'raps, if I heard a voice say, "Sam!" . . .
  Morning would find me gone.'

               *Walter de la Mare*

# One Friday Morn

One Friday morn when we set sail,
  Not very far from land,
We there did espy a fair pretty maid
  With a comb and a glass in her hand, her hand, her
      hand,
  With a comb and a glass in her hand.

    *While the raging seas did roar,*
      *And the stormy winds did blow,*
    *While we jolly sailor-boys were up into the top,*
    *And the land-lubbers lying down below, below, be-*
        *low,*
    *And the land-lubbers lying down below.*

Then up starts the captain of our gallant ship,
  And a brave young man was he:
"I've a wife and a child in fair Bristol town,
  But a widow I fear she will be."
    *And the raging seas did roar,*
      *And the stormy winds did blow.*

Then up starts the mate of our gallant ship,
  And a bold young man was he:

"Oh! I have a wife in fair Portsmouth town,
  But a widow I fear she will be."
    *And the raging seas did roar,*
      *And the stormy winds did blow.*

Then up starts the cook of our gallant ship,
  And a gruff old soul was he:
"Oh! I have a wife in fair Plymouth town,
  But a widow I fear she will be."
    *And the raging seas did roar,*
      *And the stormy winds did blow.*

And then up spoke the little cabin-boy,
  And a pretty little boy was he:
"Oh! I am more grieved for my daddy and my mammy
  Than you for your wives all three."
    *And the raging seas did roar,*
      *And the stormy winds did blow.*

Then three times round went our gallant ship,
  And three times round went she;
And three times round went our gallant ship,
  And she sank to the bottom of the sea . . .

    *And the raging seas did roar,*
      *And the stormy winds did blow.*
    *While we jolly sailor-boys were up into the top,*
      *And the land-lubbers lying down below, below, be-*
      *low,*
    *And the land-lubbers lying down below.*

*Traditional: English*

# The Lotos-Eaters

"Courage!" he said, and pointed toward the land,
"This mounting wave will roll us shoreward soon."
In the afternoon they came unto a land
In which it seemèd always afternoon.
All round the coast the languid air did swoon,
Breathing like one that hath a weary dream.
Full-faced above the valley stood the moon;
And, like a downward smoke, the slender stream
Along the cliff to fall and pause and fall did seem.

A land of streams! some, like a downward smoke,
Slow-dropping veils of thinnest lawn, did go;
And some through wavering lights and shadows broke,
Rolling a slumberous sheet of foam below.
They saw the gleaming river seaward flow
From the inner land: far off, three mountain-tops,
Three silent pinnacles of agèd snow,
Stood sunset-flushed; and, dewed with showery drops,
Up-clomb the shadowy pine above the woven copse.

The charmèd sunset lingered low adown
In the red West: through mountain clefts the dale
Was seen far inland, and the yellow down
Bordered with palm, and many a winding vale

And meadow, set with slender galingale;
A land where all things always seemed the same!
And round about the keel with faces pale,
Dark faces pale against that rosy flame,
The mild-eyed melancholy Lotos-eaters came.

Branches they bore of that enchanted stem,
Laden with flower and fruit, whereof they gave
To each, but whoso did receive of them
And taste, to him the gushing of the wave
Far, far away did seem to mourn and rave
On alien shores; and if his fellow spake,
His voice was thin, as voices from the grave;
And deep-asleep he seemed, yet all awake,
And music in his ears his beating heart did make.

They sat them down upon the yellow sand,
Between the sun and moon upon the shore;
And sweet it was to dream of Fatherland,
Of child, and wife, and slave; but evermore
Most weary seemed the sea, weary the oar,
Weary the wandering fields of barren foam.
Then some one said, "We will return no more";
And all at once they sang, "Our island home
Is far beyond the wave; we will no longer roam."

*Alfred Tennyson*

# The Listeners

"Is there anybody there?" said the Traveller,
  Knocking on the moonlit door;
And his horse in the silence champed the grasses
  Of the forest's ferny floor:
And a bird flew up out of the turret,
  Above the Traveller's head:
And he smote upon the door again a second time;
  "Is there anybody there?" he said.
But no one descended to the Traveller;
  No head from the leaf-fringed sill
Leaned over and looked into his gray eyes,
  Where he stood perplexed and still.
But only a host of phantom listeners
  That dwelt in the lone house then
Stood listening in the quiet of the moonlight
  To that voice from the world of men:
Stood thronging the faint moonbeams on the dark stair,
  That goes down to the empty hall,
Hearkening in an air stirred and shaken
  By the lonely Traveller's call.
And he felt in his heart their strangeness,
  Their stillness answering his cry,
While his horse moved, cropping the dark turf,
  'Neath the starred and leafy sky;

For he suddenly smote on the door, even
   Louder, and lifted his head:—
"Tell them I came, and no one answered,
   That I kept my word," he said.
Never the least stir made the listeners,
   Though every word he spake
Fell echoing through the shadowiness of the still house
   From the one man left awake:
Ay, they heard his foot upon the stirrup,
   And the sound of iron on stone,
And how the silence surged softly backward,
   When the plunging hoofs were gone.

*Walter de la Mare*

# The Horse Thief

There he moved, cropping the grass at the purple canyon's
    lip.
His mane was mixed with the moonlight that silvered his
    snow-white side,
For the moon sailed out of a cloud with the wake of a
    spectral ship.
I crouched and I crawled on my belly, my lariat coil
    looped wide.

Dimly and dark the mesas broke on the starry sky.
A pall covered every color of their gorgeous glory at noon.
I smelt the yucca and mesquite, and stifled my heart's
    quick cry,
And wormed and crawled on my belly to where he moved
    against the moon!

Some Moorish barb was that mustang's sire. His lines
    were beyond all wonder.
From the prick of his ears to the flow of his tail he ached
    in my throat and eyes.
Steel and velvet grace! As the prophet says, God had
    "clothed his neck with thunder."
Oh, marvelous with the drifting cloud he drifted across
    the skies!

And then I was near at hand—crouched, and balanced, and cast the coil;
And the moon was smothered in cloud, and the rope through my hands with a rip!
But somehow I gripped and clung, with the blood in my brain aboil—
With a turn round the rugged tree-stump there on the purple canyon's lip.

Right into the stars he reared aloft, his red eye rolling and raging.
He whirled and sunfished and lashed, and rocked the earth to thunder and flame.
He squealed like a regular devil horse. I was haggard and spent and aging—
Roped clean, but almost storming clear, his fury too fierce to tame.

And I cursed myself for a tenderfoot moon-dazzled to play the part;
But I was doubly desperate then, with the posse pulled out from town,
Or I'd never have tried it. I only knew I must get a mount and a start.
The filly had snapped her foreleg short—I had had to shoot her down.

So there he struggled and strangled, and I snubbed him around the tree.
Nearer, a little nearer—hoofs planted, and lolling tongue—

Till a sudden slack pitched me backward. He reared right
  on top of me.
Mother of God—that moment! He missed me . . . and
  up I swung.

Somehow, gone daft completely and clawing a bunch of
  his mane,
As he stumbled and tripped in the lariat, there I was—up
  and astride
And cursing for seven counties! And the mustang? *Just
  insane!*
Crack-bang! went the rope; we cannoned off the tree;
  then—gods, that ride!

A rocket—that's all, a rocket! I dug with my teeth and
  nails.
Why, we never hit even the high spots (though I hardly
  remember things);
But I heard a monstrous booming like a thunder of flap-
  ping sails
When he spread—well, *call* me a liar!—when he spread
  those wings, those wings!

So white that my eyes were blinded; thick-feathered and
  wide unfurled,
They beat the air into billows. We sailed, and the earth
  was gone.
Canyon and desert and mesa withered below, with the
  world.
And then I knew that mustang; for I—was Bellerophon!

Yes, glad as the Greek, and mounted on a horse of the
    elder gods,
With never a magic bridle or a fountain-mirror nigh!
*My chaps and spurs and holster must have looked it?
    What's the odds?*
I'd a leg over lightning and thunder, careering across the
    sky!

And forever streaming before me, fanning my forehead
    cool,
Flowed a mane of molten silver; and just before my
    thighs
(As I gripped his velvet-muscled ribs, while I cursed my-
    self for a fool),
The steady pulse of those pinions—their wonderful fall
    and rise!

The bandanna I bought in Bowie blew loose and whipped
    from my neck.
My shirt was stuck to my shoulders and ribboning out be-
    hind.
The stars were dancing, wheeling and glancing, dipping
    with smirk and beck.
The clouds were flowing, dusking and glowing. We rode
    a roaring wind.

We soared through the silver starlight to knock at the
    planets' gates.
New shimmering constellations came whirling into our
    ken.

Red stars and green and golden swung out of the void that
    waits
For man's great last adventure; the Signs took shape—and
    then

I knew the lines of that Centaur the moment I saw him
    come!
The musical-box of the heavens all around us rolled to a
    tune
That tinkled and chimed and trilled with silver sounds
    that struck you dumb,
As if some archangel were grinding out the music of the
    moon.

Melody-drunk on the Milky Way, as we swept and soared
    hilarious,
Full in our pathway, sudden he stood—the Centaur of the
    Stars,
Flashing from head and hoofs and breast! I knew him for
    Sagittarius.
He reared, and bent and drew his bow. He crouched as a
    boxer spars.

Flung back on his haunches, weird he loomed; then leapt
    —and the dim void lightened.
Old White Wings shied and swerved aside, and fled from
    the splendor-shod.
Through a flashing welter of worlds we charged. I knew
    why my horse was frightened.
He *had* two faces—a dog's and a man's—that Babylonian
    god!

304

Also, he followed us real as fear. Ping! went an arrow past.
My broncho buck-jumped, humping high. We plunged
. . . I guess that's all!
I lay on the purple canyon's lip, when I opened my eyes at
last—
Stiff and sore and my head like a drum, but I broke no
bones in the fall.

So you know—and now you may string me up. Such was
the way you caught me.
Thank you for letting me tell it straight, though you
never could greatly care.
For I took a horse that wasn't mine! . . . But there's one
the heavens brought me,
And I'll hang right happy because I know he is waiting for
me up there.

From creamy muzzle to cannon-bone, by God, he's a peer-
less wonder!
He is steel and velvet and furnace-fire, and death's su-
premest prize;
And never again shall be roped on earth that neck that is
"clothed in thunder" . . .
String me up, Dave! Go dig my grave! *I rode him across
the skies!*

*William Rose Benét*

# Birds and Beasts

# The Birds of Killingworth

It was the season, when through all the land
    The merle and mavis build, and building sing
Those lovely lyrics, written by His hand,
    Whom Saxon Caedmon calls the Blithe-heart King;
When on the boughs the purple buds expand,
    The banners of the vanguard of the Spring,
And rivulets, rejoicing, rush and leap,
And wave their fluttering signals from the steep.

The robin and the blue-bird, piping loud,
    Filled all the blossoming orchards with their glee;
The sparrows chirped as if they still were proud
    Their race in Holy Writ should mentioned be;
And hungry crows assembled in a crowd,
    Clamored their piteous prayer incessantly,
Knowing who hears the ravens cry, and said:
"Give us, O Lord, this day our daily bread!"

Across the Sound the birds of passage sailed,
    Speaking some unknown language strange and sweet
Of tropic isle remote, and passing hailed
    The village with the cheers of all their fleet;

Or quarrelling together, laughed and railed
  Like foreign sailors, landed in the street
Of seaport town, and with outlandish noise
Of oaths and gibberish frightening girls and boys.

Thus came the jocund Spring in Killingworth,
  In fabulous days, some hundred years ago;
And thrifty farmers, as they tilled the earth,
  Heard with alarm the cawing of the crow,
That mingled with the universal mirth,
  Cassandra-like, prognosticating woe;
They shook their heads, and doomed with dreadful **words**
To swift destruction the whole race of birds.

And a town-meeting was convened straightway
  To set a price upon the guilty heads
Of these marauders, who, in lieu of pay,
  Levied blackmail upon the garden beds
And cornfields, and beheld without dismay
  The awful scarecrow, with his fluttering shreds;
The skeleton that waited at their feast,
Whereby their sinful pleasure was increased.

Then from his house, a temple painted white,
  With fluted columns, and a roof of red,
The Squire came forth, august and splendid sight!
  Slowly descending, with majestic tread,
Three flights of steps, nor looking left nor right,
  Down the long street he walked, as one who said,
"A town that boasts inhabitants like me
Can have no lack of good society!"

309

The Parson, too, appeared, a man austere,
　　The instinct of whose nature was to kill;
The wrath of God he preached from year to year,
　　And read, with fervor, Edwards on the Will;
His favorite pastime was to slay the deer
　　In Summer on some Adirondack hill;
E'en now, while walking down the rural lane,
He lopped the wayside lilies with his cane.

From the Academy, whose belfry crowned
　　The hill of Science with its vane of brass,
Came the Preceptor, gazing idly round,
　　Now at the clouds, and now at the green grass,
And all absorbed in reveries profound
　　Of fair Almira in the upper class,
Who was, as in a sonnet he had said,
As pure as water, and as good as bread.

And next the Deacon issued from his door,
　　In his voluminous neck-cloth, white as snow;
A suit of sable bombazine he wore;
　　His form was ponderous, and his step was slow;
There never was so wise a man before;
　　He seemed the incarnate "Well, I told you so!"
And to perpetuate his great renown
There was a street named after him in town.

These came together in the new townhall,
　　With sundry farmers from the region round.
The Squire presided, dignified and tall,
　　His air impressive and his reasoning sound;

Ill fared it with the birds, both great and small;
  Hardly a friend in all that crowd they found,
But enemies enough, who every one
Charged them with all the crimes beneath the sun.

When they had ended, from his place apart,
  Rose the Preceptor, to redress the wrong,
And, trembling like a steed before the start,
  Looked round bewildered on the expectant throng;
Then thought of fair Almira, and took heart
  To speak out what was in him, clear and strong,
Alike regardless of their smile or frown,
And quite determined not to be laughed down.

"Plato, anticipating the Reviewers,
  From his republic banished without pity
The Poets; in this little town of yours,
  You put to death, by means of a Committee,
The ballad-singers and the Troubadours,
  The street-musicians of the heavenly city,
The birds, who make sweet music for us all
In our dark hours, as David did for Saul.

"The thrush that carols at the dawn of day
  From the green steeples of the piny wood;
The oriole in the elm; the noisy jay,
  Jargoning like a foreigner for his food;
The blue-bird balanced on some topmost spray,
  Flooding with melody the neighborhood;
Linnet and meadow-lark, and all the throng
That dwell in nests, and have the gift of song.

"You slay them all! and wherefore? for the gain
    Of a scant handful more or less of wheat,
Or rye, or barley, or some other grain,
    Scratched up at random by industrious feet,
Searching for worm or weevil after rain!
    Of a few cherries, that are not so sweet
As are the songs these uninvited guests
Sing at their feast with comfortable breasts.

"Do you ne'er think what wondrous beings these?
    Do you ne'er think who made them, and who taught
The dialect they speak, where melodies
    Alone are the interpreters of thought?
Whose household words are songs in many keys,
    Sweeter than instrument of man e'er caught!
Whose habitations in the tree-tops even
Are half-way houses on the road to heaven!

"Think, every morning when the sun peeps through
    The dim, leaf-latticed windows of the grove,
How jubilant the happy birds renew
    Their old, melodious madrigals of love!
And when you think of this, remember too
    'T is always morning somewhere, and above
The awakening continents, from shore to shore,
Somewhere the birds are singing evermore.

"Think of your woods and orchards without birds!
    Of empty nests that cling to boughs and beams
As in an idiot's brain remembered words
    Hang empty 'mid the cobwebs of his dreams!

Will bleat of flocks or bellowing of herds
   Make up for the lost music, when your teams
Drag home the stingy harvest, and no more
The feathered gleaners follow to your door?

"What! would you rather see the incessant stir
   Of insects in the windrows of the hay,
And hear the locust and the grasshopper
   Their melancholy hurdy-gurdies play?
Is this more pleasant to you than the whir
   Of meadow-lark, and her sweet roundelay,
Or twitter of little field-fares, as you take
Your nooning in the shade of bush and brake?

"You call them thieves and pillagers; but know,
   They are the winged wardens of your farms,
Who from the cornfields drive the insidious foe,
   And from your harvest keep a hundred harms;
Even the blackest of them all, the crow,
   Renders good service as your man-at-arms,
Crushing the beetle in his coat of mail,
And crying havoc on the slug and snail.

"How can I teach your children gentleness,
   And mercy to the weak, and reverence
For life which, in its weakness or excess,
   Is still a gleam of God's omnipotence,
Or Death which, seeming darkness, is no less
   The selfsame light, although averted hence,
When by your laws, your actions, and your speech
You contradict the very things I teach?"

With this he closed; and through the audience went
    A murmur, like the rustle of dead leaves;
The farmers laughed and nodded and some bent
    Their yellow heads together like their sheaves;
Men have no faith in fine-spun sentiment
    Who put their trust in bullocks and in beeves.
The birds were doomed; and, as the record shows,
A bounty offered for the heads of crows.

There was another audience out of reach,
    Who had no voice nor vote in making laws,
But in the papers read his little speech,
    And crowned his modest temples with applause;
They made him conscious, each one more than each,
    He still was victor, vanquished in their cause.
Sweetest of all the applause he won from thee,
O fair Almira of the Academy!

And so the dreadful massacre began
    O'er fields and orchards, and o'er woodland crests,
The ceaseless fusillade of terror ran,
    Dead fell the birds, with blood-stains on their breasts,
Or wounded crept away from sight of man,
    While the young died of famine in their nests;
A slaughter to be told in groans, not words,
The very St. Bartholomew of Birds!

The summer came, and all the birds were dead;
    The days were like hot coals; the very ground
Was burned to ashes; in the orchards fed
    Myriads of caterpillars, and around

The cultivated fields and garden beds
 Hosts of devouring insects crawled, and found
No foe to check their march, till they had made
The land a desert without leaf or shade.

Devoured by worms, like Herod, was the town,
 Because, like Herod, it had ruthlessly
Slaughtered the Innocents. From the trees spun down
 The canker-worms upon the passersby,
Upon each woman's bonnet, shawl, and gown,
 Who shook them off with just a little cry;
They were the terror of each favorite walk,
The endless theme of all the village talk.

The farmers grew impatient, but a few
 Confessed their error, and would not complain,
For after all, the best thing one can do
 When it is raining, is to let it rain.
Then they repealed the law, although they knew
 It would not call the dead to life again;
As school-boys, finding their mistake too late,
Draw a wet sponge across the accusing slate.

That year in Killingworth the Autumn came
 Without the light of his majestic look,
The wonder of the falling tongues of flame
 The illumined pages of his Doomsday book.
A few lost leaves blushed crimson with their shame,
 And drowned themselves despairing in the brook,
While the wild wind went moaning everywhere,
Lamenting the dead children of the air!

But the next Spring a stranger sight was seen,
  A sight that never yet by bard was sung,
As great a wonder as it would have been
  If some dumb animal had found a tongue!
A wagon, overarched with evergreen,
  Upon whose boughs were wicker cages hung,
All full of singing birds, came down the street,
Filling the air with music wild and sweet.

From all the country round these birds were brought,
  By order of the town, with anxious quest,
And, loosened from their wicker prisons, sought
  In woods and fields the places they loved best,
Singing loud canticles, which many thought
  Were satires to the authorities addressed,
While others, listening in green lanes, averred
Such lovely music never had been heard!

But blither still and louder carolled they
  Upon the morrow, for they seemed to know
It was the fair Almira's wedding day,
  And everywhere, around, above, below,
When the Preceptor bore his bride away,
  Their songs burst forth in joyous overflow,
And a new heaven bent over a new earth
Amid the sunny farms of Killingworth.

*Henry Wadsworth Longfellow*

# A Legend of the Northland

Away, away in the Northland,
   Where the hours of day are few,
And the nights are so long in winter
   That they cannot sleep them through;

There they harness the swift reindeer
   To the sledges when it snows;
And the children look like bear's cubs
   In their funny, furry clothes:

They tell them a curious story—
   I don't believe 'tis true;
And yet you may learn a lesson
   If I tell the tale to you.

Once, when the good Saint Peter
   Lived in the world below,
And walked about it, preaching,
   Just as he did, you know,

He came to the door of a cottage,
   In traveling round the earth,
Where a little woman was making cakes,
   And baking them on the hearth;

And being faint with fasting,
  For the day was almost done,
He asked her, from her store of cakes,
  To give him a single one.


So she made a very little cake,
  But as it baking lay,
She looked at it, and thought it seemed
  Too large to give away.


Therefore she kneaded another,
  And still a smaller one;
But it looked, when she turned it over,
  As large as the first had done.


Then she took a tiny scrap of dough,
  And rolled and rolled it flat;
And baked it thin as a wafer—
  But she couldn't part with that.


For she said, "My cakes that seem too small
  When I eat of them myself,
Are yet too large to give away."
  So she put them on the shelf.


Then good Saint Peter grew angry,
  For he was hungry and faint;
And surely such a woman
  Was enough to provoke a saint.

And he said, "You are far too selfish
  To dwell in a human form,
To have both food and shelter,
  And fire to keep you warm.

"Now, you shall build as the birds do,
  And shall get your scanty food
By boring, and boring, and boring,
  All day in the hard dry wood."

Then up she went through the chimney,
  Never speaking a word,
And out of the top flew a woodpecker,
  For she was changed to a bird.

She had a scarlet cap on her head,
  And that was left the same,
But all the rest of her clothes were burned
  Black as a coal in the flame.

And every country schoolboy
  Had seen her in the wood,
Where she lives in the trees till this very day,
  Boring and boring for food.

*Phoebe Cary*

319

# The Nightingale and the Glowworm

A Nightingale that all day long
Had cheer'd the village with his song,
Nor yet at eve his note suspended,
Nor yet when eventide was ended,
Began to feel, as well he might,
The keen demands of appetite;
When looking eagerly around,
He spied far off, upon the ground,
A something shining in the dark,
And knew the Glowworm by his spark;
So, stooping down from hawthorn top,
He thought to put him in his crop.
The worm, aware of his intent,
Harangued him thus, right eloquent:
"Did you admire my lamp," quoth he,
"As much as I your minstrelsy,
You would abhor to do me wrong,
As much as I to spoil your song:
For 'twas the self-same Power Divine
Taught you to sing, and me to shine;
That you with music, I with light,
Might beautify and cheer the night."

The songster heard this short oration,
And warbling out his approbation,
Released him, as my story tells,
And found a supper somewhere else.

*William  Cowper*

# The Jackdaw of Rheims

The Jackdaw sat on the Cardinal's chair:
Bishop and abbot and prior were there,
> Many a monk, and many a friar,
> Many a knight, and many a squire,
With a great many more of lesser degree,—
In sooth, a goodly company;
And they served the Lord Primate on bended knee.
> Never, I ween,
> Was a prouder seen,
Read of in books, or dreamt of in dreams,
Than the Cardinal Lord Archbishop of Rheims!

> In and out
> Through the motley rout,
That little Jackdaw kept hopping about;
> Here and there
> Like a dog in a fair,
> Over comfits and cates,
> And dishes and plates,
Cowl and cope, and rochet and pall,
Mitre and crosier, he hopped upon all!
> With a saucy air,
> He perched on the chair
Where, in state, the great Lord Cardinal sat,
In the great Lord Cardinal's great red hat;

    And he peered in the face
    Of his Lordship's Grace,
With a satisfied look, as if he would say,
"We two are the greatest folks here to-day!"
    And the priests, with awe,
    As such freaks they saw,
Said, "The Devil must be in that little Jackdaw!"

The feast was over, the board was cleared,
The flawns and the custards had all disappeared,
And six little Singing-boys,—dear little souls!
In nice clean faces, and nice white stoles,—
    Came in order due,
    Two by two,
Marching that grand refectory through.
A nice little boy held a golden ewer,
Embossed and filled with water, as pure
As any that flows between Rheims and Namur
Which a nice little boy stood ready to catch
In a fine golden hand-basin made to match.
Two nice little boys, rather more grown,
Carried lavender-water and eau-de-Cologne;
And a nice little boy had a nice cake of soap,
Worthy of washing the hands of the Pope.
    One little boy more
    A napkin bore,
Of the best white diaper, fringed with pink,
And a Cardinal's hat marked in "permanent ink."

The great Lord Cardinal turns at the sight
Of these nice little boys dressed all in white:

From his finger he draws
   His costly turquoise;
And, not thinking at all about little Jackdaws,
   Deposits it straight
   By the side of his plate,
While the nice little boys on his Eminence wait;
Till, when nobody's dreaming of any such thing,
That little Jackdaw hops off with the ring!

.     .     .     .     .     .

   There's a cry and a shout,
   And a deuce of a rout,
And nobody seems to know what they're about,
But the monks have their pockets all turned inside out;
   The friars are kneeling,
   And hunting, and feeling
The carpet, the floor, and the walls, and the ceiling.
   The Cardinal drew
   Off each plum-colored shoe,
And left his red stockings exposed to the view;
   He peeps, and he feels
   In the toes and the heels;
They turn up the dishes,—they turn up the plates,—
They take up the poker and poke out the grates,
   —They turn up the rugs,
   They examine the mugs:
   But no!—no such thing;
   They can't find THE RING!
And the Abbot declared that, "When nobody twigged it,
Some rascal or other had popped in and prigged it!"

The Cardinal rose with a dignified look,
He called for his candle, his bell, and his book:
In holy anger, and pious grief,
He solemnly cursed that rascally thief!
He cursed him at board, he cursed him in bed,
From the sole of his foot to the crown of his head!
He cursed him in sleeping, that every night
He should dream of the devil, and wake in a fright;
He cursed him in eating, he cursed him in drinking,
He cursed him in coughing, in sneezing, in winking;
He cursed him in sitting, in standing, in lying;
He cursed him in walking, in riding, in flying;
He cursed him in living, he cursed him in dying!
Never was heard such a terrible curse!
But what gave rise
To no little surprise,
Nobody seemed one penny the worse!


The day was gone,
The night came on,
The monks and the friars they searched till dawn;
When the sacristan saw,
On crumpled claw
Come limping a poor little lame Jackdaw.
No longer gay,
As on yesterday;
His feathers all seemed to be turned the wrong way;
His pinions drooped—he could hardly stand,
His head was as bald as the palm of your hand;
His eye so dim,
So wasted each limb,

That, heedless of grammar, they all cried, "THAT'S
    HIM.
That's the scamp that has done this scandalous thing!
That's the thief that has got my Lord Cardinal's **Ring!**"
    The poor little Jackdaw,
    When the monks he saw,
Feebly gave vent to the ghost of a caw;
And turned his bald head, as much as to **say,**
"Pray, be so good as to walk this way!"
    Slower and slower
    He limped on before,
Till they came to the back of the belfry-door,
    Where the first thing they saw,
    Midst the sticks and the straw,
Was the RING, in the nest of that little Jackdaw.


Then the great Lord Cardinal called for his book,
And off that terrible curse he took;
    The mute expression
    Served in lieu of confession,
And, being thus coupled with full restitution,
The Jackdaw got plenary absolution!
    —When those words were heard,
    That poor little bird
Was so changed in a moment, 'twas really absurd.
    He grew sleek and fat;
    In addition to that,
A fresh crop of feathers came thick as a mat.
    His tail waggled more
    Even than before;

But no longer it wagged with an impudent air,
No longer he perched on the Cardinal's chair.
    He hopped now about
    With a gait devout;
At matins, at vespers, he never was out;
And, so far from any more pilfering deeds,
He always seemed telling the Confessor's beads.
If any one lied, or if any one swore,
Or slumbered in prayer-time, and happened to snore,
    That good Jackdaw
    Would give a great "Caw!"
As much as to say, "Don't do so any more!"
While many remarked, as his manner they saw,
That they "never had known such a pious Jackdaw!"

    He long lived the pride
    Of that country side,
And at last in the odor of sanctity died;
    When, as words were too faint
    His merits to paint,
The Conclave determined to make him a Saint;
And on newly-made Saints and Popes, as you know,
It's the custom, at Rome, new names to bestow,
So they canonized him by the name of Jem Crow!

*Richard Harris Barham*

# The Lion and the Mouse

A lion with the heat oppressed,
One day composed himself to rest:
But while he dozed as he intended,
A mouse, his royal back ascended;
Nor thought of harm, as Aesop tells,
Mistaking him for someone else;
And travelled over him, and round him,
And might have left him as she found him
Had she not—tremble when you hear—
Tried to explore the monarch's ear!
Who straightway woke, with wrath immense,
And shook his head to cast her thence.
"You rascal, what are you about?"
Said he, when he had turned her out,
"I'll teach you soon," the lion said,
"To make a mouse-hole in my head!"
So saying, he prepared his foot
To crush the trembling tiny brute;
But she (the mouse) with tearful eye,
Implored the lion's clemency,
Who thought it best at last to give
His little prisoner a reprieve.

'Twas nearly twelve months after this
The lion chanced his way to miss;

When pressing forward, heedless yet,
He got entangled in a net.
With dreadful rage, he stamped and tore,
And straight commenced a lordly roar;
When the poor mouse, who heard the noise
Attended, for she knew his voice.
Then what the lion's utmost strength
Could not effect, she did at length;
With patient labor she applied
Her teeth, the network to divide;
And so at last forth issued he,
A *lion,* by a mouse set free.

Few are so small or weak, I guess,
But may assist us in distress,
Nor shall we ever, if we're wise,
The meanest, or the least despise.

*Jeffreys Taylor*

# The Blind Men and the Elephant

## A HINDOO FABLE

It was six men of Indostan
  To learning much inclined,
Who went to see the Elephant
  (Though all of them were blind),
That each by observation
  Might satisfy his mind.

The *First* approached the Elephant,
  And happening to fall
Against his broad and sturdy side,
  At once began to bawl:
"God bless me! but the Elephant
  Is very like a wall!"

The *Second*, feeling of the tusk,
  Cried, "Ho! what have we here
So very round and smooth and sharp?
  To me 'tis mighty clear
This wonder of an Elephant
  Is very like a spear!"

The *Third* approached the animal
  And happening to take

The squirming trunk within his hands,
    Thus boldly up and spake:
"I see," quoth he, "the Elephant
    Is very like a snake!"

The *Fourth* reached out an eager hand,
    And felt about the knee.
"What most this wondrous beast is like
    Is mighty plain," quoth he;
" 'Tis clear enough the Elephant
    Is very like a tree!"

The *Fifth* who chanced to touch the ear,
    Said: "E'en the blindest man
Can tell what this resembles most;
    Deny the fact who can,
This marvel of an Elephant
    Is very like a fan!"

The *Sixth* no sooner had begun
    About the beast to grope,
Than, seizing on the swinging tail
    That fell within his scope,
"I see," quoth he, "the Elephant
    Is very like a rope!"

And so these men of Indostan
    Disputed loud and long,
Each in his own opinion
    Exceeding stiff and strong,
Though each was partly in the right,
    And all were in the wrong!

THE MORAL

So oft in theologic wars,
  The disputants, I ween,
Rail on in utter ignorance
  Of what each other mean,
*And prate about an Elephant*
  *Not one of them has seen!*

John  Godfrey  Saxe

# Fable

The mountain and the squirrel
Had a quarrel,
And the former called the latter "Little Prig";
Bun replied,
"You are doubtless very big;
But all sorts of things and weather
Must be taken in together,
To make up a year
And a sphere.
And I think it no disgrace
To occupy my place.
If I'm not so large as you,
You are not so small as I,
And not half so spry.

I'll not deny you make
A very pretty squirrel track;
Talents differ; all is well and wisely put;
If I cannot carry forests on my back,
Neither can you crack a nut."

*Ralph Waldo Emerson*

# The Virtuous Fox and the Self-Righteous Cat

The fox and the cat, as they travell'd one day,
With moral discourses cut shorter the way:
" 'Tis great," says the Fox, "to make justice our guide!"
"How god-like is mercy!" Grimalkin replied.

Whilst thus they proceeded, a wolf from the wood,
Impatient of hunger, and thirsting for blood,
Rush'd forth—as he saw the dull shepherd asleep—
And seiz'd for his supper an innocent sheep.
"In vain, wretched victim, for mercy you bleat,
When mutton's at hand," says the wolf, "I must eat."

Grimalkin's astonish'd!—the fox stood aghast,
To see the fell beast at his bloody repast.
"What a wretch," says the cat, " 'tis the vilest of brutes;
Does he feed upon flesh when there's herbage and roots?"
Cries the fox, "While our oaks give us acorns so good,
What a tyrant is this to spill innocent blood!"

Well, onward they march'd, and they moraliz'd still,
Till they came where some poultry pick'd chaff by a mill
Sly Reynard survey'd them with gluttonous eyes,
And made, spite of morals, a pullet his prize.
A mouse, too, that chanc'd from her covert to stray,
The greedy Grimalkin secured as her prey.

A spider that sat in her web on the wall,
Perceiv'd the poor victims, and pitied their fall;
She cried, "Of such murders, how guiltless am I!"
So ran to regale on a new-taken fly.

*John Cunningham*

# Old Mother Hubbard

Old Mother Hubbard
Went to the cupboard
To get her poor dog a bone:
But when she got there
The cupboard was bare,
And so the poor dog had none.

She went to the baker's
To buy him some bread,
But when she came back
The poor dog was dead.

She went to the joiner's
To buy him a coffin,
But when she came back
The poor dog was laughing.

She took a clean dish
To get him some tripe,
But when she came back
He was smoking a pipe.

She went to the fishmonger's
To buy him some fish,

But when she came back
    He was licking the dish.


She went to the tavern
    For white wine and red,
But when she came back
    The dog stood on his head.


She went to the hatter's
    To buy him a hat,
But when she came back
    He was feeding the cat.


She went to the barber's
    To buy him a wig,
But when she came back
    He was dancing a jig.


She went to the fruiterer's
    To buy him some fruit,
But when she came back
    He was playing the flute.


She went to the tailor's
    To buy him a coat,
But when she came back
    He was riding a goat.


She went to the cobbler's
    To buy him some shoes,

But when she came back
    He was reading the news.

She went to the seamstress
    To buy him some linen,
But when she came back
    The dog was spinning.

She went to the hosier's
    To buy him some hose,
But when she came back
    He was dressed in his clothes.

The dame made a curtsey,
    The dog made a bow,
The dame said, "Your servant,"
    The dog said, "Bow-wow."

This wonderful dog
    Was Dame Hubbard's delight;
He could sing, he could dance,
    He could read, he could write.

She gave him rich dainties
    Whenever he fed,
And built him a monument
    When he was dead.

*Traditional: English*

# A Frog He Would A-Wooing Go

A frog he would a-wooing go,
   *Heigho, says Rowley,*
Whether his mother would let him or no.
   *With a rowley powley, gammon and spinach,*
   *Heigho, says Anthony Rowley!*

So off he·set with his opera hat,
   *Heigho, says Rowley,*
And on the road he met with a rat.
   *With a rowley powley, gammon and spinach,*
   *Heigho, says Anthony Rowley!*

"Pray, Mr. Rat, will you go with me,
   *Heigho, says Rowley,*
Kind Mrs. Mousey for to see?"
   *With a rowley powley, gammon and spinach,*
   *Heigho, says Anthony Rowley!*

When they came to the door of Mousey's hall,
   *Heigho, says Rowley,*
They gave a loud knock and they gave a loud call.
   *With a rowley powley, gammon and spinach,*
   *Heigho, says Anthony Rowley!*

"Pray, Mrs. Mouse, are you within?"
*Heigho, says Rowley,*
"Oh, yes, kind sirs, I'm sitting to spin."
*With a rowley powley, gammon and spinach,*
*Heigho, says Anthony Rowley!*


"Pray, Mrs. Mouse, will you give us some beer?
*Heigho, says Rowley,*
For Froggy and I are fond of good cheer."
*With a rowley powley, gammon and spinach,*
*Heigho, says Anthony Rowley!*


"Pray, Mr. Frog, will you give us a song?
*Heigho, says Rowley,*
But let it be something that's not very long."
*With a rowley powley, gammon and spinach,*
*Heigho, says Anthony Rowley!*


"Indeed, **Mrs. Mouse,**" replied the frog,
*Heigho, says Rowley,*
"A cold has made me as hoarse as a dog."
*With a rowley powley, gammon and spinach,*
*Heigho, says Anthony Rowley!*


"Since you have caught cold, Mr. Frog," Mousey said,
*Heigho, says Rowley,*
"I'll sing you a song that I have just made."
*With a rowley powley, gammon and spinach,*
*Heigho, says Anthony Rowley!*

But while they were making a merry din,
  *Heigho, says Rowley,*
A cat and her kittens came tumbling in.
  *With a rowley powley, gammon and spinach,*
  *Heigho, says Anthony Rowley!*

The cat she seized the rat by the crown;
  *Heigho, says Rowley,*
The kittens they pulled the little mouse down.
  *With a rowley powley, gammon and spinach,*
  *Heigho, says Anthony Rowley!*

This put Mr. Frog in a terrible fright,
  *Heigho, says Rowley,*
He took up his hat, and he wished them good night.
  *With a rowley powley, gammon and spinach,*
  *Heigho, says Anthony Rowley!*

But as Froggy was crossing over a brook,
  *Heigho, says Rowley,*
A lily-white duck came and gobbled him up.
  *With a rowley powley, gammon and spinach,*
  *Heigho, says Anthony Rowley!*

So there was an end of one, two, and three,
  *Heigho, says Rowley,*
The Rat, the Mouse, and the little Frog-gee!
  *With a rowley powley, gammon and spinach,*
  *Heigho, says Anthony Rowley!*

*Old English Song*

341

# The Butterfly and the Caterpillar

A FABLE OLD IS HERE RETOLD

A butterfly, one summer morn,
Sat on a spray of blossoming thorn
And, as he sipped and drank his share
Of honey from the flowered air,
Below, upon the garden wall,
A caterpillar chanced to crawl.
"Horrors!" the butterfly exclaimed,
"This must be stopped! I am ashamed
That such as I should have to be
In the same world with such as he.
Preserve me from such hideous things!
Disgusting shape! Where are his wings!
Fuzzy and gray! Eater of clay!
Won't someone take the worm away!"

The caterpillar crawled ahead,
But, as he munched a leaf, he said,
"Eight days ago, young butterfly,
You wormed about, the same as I;
Within a fortnight from today
Two wings will bear me far away,
To brighter blooms and lovelier lures,
With colors that outrival yours.

342

So, flutter-flit, be not so proud;
Each caterpillar is endowed
With power to make him by and by,
A blithe and brilliant butterfly.
While you, who scorn the common clay,
You, in your livery so gay,
And all the gaudy moths and millers,
Are only dressed-up caterpillars."

*Joseph Lauren*

# Christmastide

# A Visit from St. Nicholas

'Twas the night before Christmas, when all through the
      house
Not a creature was stirring, not even a mouse;
The stockings were hung by the chimney with care,
In hopes that St. Nicholas soon would be there;
The children were nestled all snug in their beds,
While visions of sugar-plums danced in their heads;
And mamma in her 'kerchief, and I in my cap,
Had just settled our brains for a long winter's nap,
When out on the lawn there arose such a clatter,
I sprang from the bed to see what was the matter.
Away to the window I flew like a flash,
Tore open the shutters and threw up the sash.
The moon on the breast of the new-fallen snow
Gave the lustre of mid-day to objects below,
When, what to my wondering eyes should appear
But a miniature sleigh, and eight tiny reindeer,
With a little old driver, so lively and quick,
I knew in a moment it must be St. Nick.
More rapid than eagles his coursers they came,
And he whistled, and shouted, and called them by name;
"Now, *Dasher!* now, *Dancer!* now, *Prancer* and *Vixen!*

On, *Comet!* on, *Cupid!* on, *Donder* and *Blitzen!*
To the top of the porch! to the top of the wall!
Now dash away! dash away! dash away all!"
As dry leaves that before the wild hurricane fly,
When they meet with an obstacle, mount to the sky,
So up to the house-tops the coursers they flew,
With the sleigh full of toys, and St. Nicholas too.
And then, in a twinkling, I heard on the roof
The prancing and pawing of each little hoof.
As I drew in my head, and was turning around,
Down the chimney St. Nicholas came with a bound.
He was dressed all in fur, from his head to his foot,
And his clothes were all tarnished with ashes and soot;
A bundle of toys he had flung on his back,
And he looked like a peddler just opening his pack.
His eyes—how they twinkled! his dimples how merry!
His cheeks were like roses, his nose like a cherry!
His droll little mouth was drawn up like a bow,
And the beard of his chin was as white as the snow;
The stump of a pipe he held tight in his teeth,
And the smoke it encircled his head like a wreath;
He had a broad face and a little round belly,
That shook, when he laughed, like a bowlful of jelly.
He was chubby and plump, a right jolly old elf,
And I laughed when I saw him, in spite of myself;
A wink of his eye and a twist of his head,
Soon gave me to know I had nothing to dread;
He spoke not a word, but went straight to his work,
And filled all the stockings; then turned with a jerk,
And laying his finger aside of his nose,

347

And giving a nod, up the chimney he rose;
He sprang to his sleigh, to his team gave a whistle,
And away they all flew like the down of a thistle.
But I heard him exclaim, ere he drove out of sight,

*"Happy Christmas to all, and to all a good-night."*

*Clement Clarke Moore*

# The Cherry-Tree Carol

Joseph was an old man,
   and an old man was he,
When he wedded Mary,
   in the land of Galilee.

Joseph and Mary walked
   through an orchard good,
Where was cherries and berries,
   so red as any blood.

Joseph and Mary walked
   through an orchard green,
Where was berries and cherries,
   as thick as might be seen.

O then bespoke Mary,
   so meek and so mild:
'Pluck me one cherry, Joseph,
   for I am with child.'

O then bespoke Joseph,
   with words most unkind:
'Let him pluck thee a cherry
   that brought thee with child.'

349

O then bespoke the babe,
  within his mother's womb:
'Bow down then the tallest tree,
  for my mother to have some.'


Then bowed down the highest tree
  unto his mother's hand;
Then she cried, 'See, Joseph,
  I have cherries at command.'


'O eat your cherries, Mary,
  O eat your cherries, now;
O eat your cherries, Mary,
  that grow upon the bough.'


As Joseph was a walking,
  he heard an angel sing:
'This night shall be born
  our heavenly king.


'He neither shall be born
  in housen nor in hall,
Nor in the place of Paradise,
  but in an ox's stall.


'He neither shall be clothed
  in purple nor in pall,
But all in fair linen,
  as were babies all.

'He neither shall be rocked
   in silver nor in gold,
But in a wooden cradle,
   that rocks on the mould.

'He neither shall be christened
   in white wine nor red,
But with fair spring water,
   with which we were christened.'

Then Mary took her babe,
   and sat him on her knee,
Saying, 'My dear son, tell me
   what this world will be.'

'O I shall be as dead, mother,
   as the stones in the wall;
O the stones in the streets, mother,
   shall mourn for me all.

'Upon Easter-day, mother,
   my uprising shall be;
O the sun and the moon, mother,
   shall both rise with me.'

*Traditional: English*

# A Christmas Folk-Song

The little Jesus came to town;
The wind blew up, the wind blew down;
Out in the street the wind was bold;
Now who would house Him from the cold?

Then opened wide a stable door,
Fair were the rushes on the floor;
The Ox put forth a hornèd head:
"Come, little Lord, here make Thy bed."

Uprose the Sheep were folded near:
"Thou Lamb of God, come, enter here."
He entered there to rush and reed,
Who was the Lamb of God indeed.

The little Jesus came to town;
With ox and sheep He laid Him down;
Peace to the byre, peace to the fold,
For that they housed Him from the cold!

*Lizette Woodworth Reese*

# The Friendly Beasts

Jesus our brother, strong and good,
Was humbly born in a stable rude,
And the friendly beasts around Him stood,
Jesus our brother, strong and good.

"I," said the donkey shaggy and brown,
"I carried His mother up hill and down,
I carried her safely to Bethlehem town;
I," said the donkey, shaggy and brown.

"I," said the cow all white and red,
"I gave Him my manger for His bed,
I gave Him my hay to pillow His head,
I," said the cow all white and red.

"I," said the sheep with curly horn,
"I gave Him my wool for His blanket warm,
He wore my coat on Christmas morn;
I," said the sheep with curly horn.

"I," said the dove, from the rafters high,
"Cooed Him to sleep, my mate and I,
We cooed Him to sleep, my mate and I;
I," said the dove, from the rafters high.

And every beast, by some good spell,
In the stable dark was glad to tell,
Of the gift he gave Immanuel,
The gift he gave Immanuel.

*Traditional: English*

# Good King Wenceslas

Good King Wenceslas looked out,
  On the Feast of Stephen,
When the snow lay round about,
  Deep, and crisp, and even:
Brightly shone the moon that night,
  Though the frost was cruel,
When a poor man came in sight,
  Gathering winter fuel.

"Hither, page, and stand by me,
  If thou know'st it, telling,
Yonder peasant, who is he?
  Where and what his dwelling?"
"Sire, he lives a good league hence,
  Underneath the mountain;
Right against the forest fence,
  By Saint Agnes' fountain."

"Bring me flesh, and bring me wine,
  Bring me pine logs hither;
Thou and I will see him dine,
  When we bear them thither."

Page and monarch forth they went,
  Forth they went together;
Through the rude wind's wild lament,
  And the bitter weather.

"Sire, the night is darker now,
  And the wind blows stronger;
Fails my heart, I know not how,
  I can go no longer."
"Mark my footsteps, good my page!
  Tread thou in them boldly;
Thou shalt find the winter's rage
  Freeze thy blood less coldly."

In his master's steps he trod,
  Where the snow lay dinted;
Heat was in the very sod
  Which the saint had printed.
Therefore, Christian men, be sure,
  Wealth or rank possessing,
Ye who now will bless the poor,
  Shall yourselves find blessing.

*John Mason Neale*

# The Three Kings

Three Kings came riding from far away,
  Melchior and Gaspar and Baltasar;
Three Wise Men out of the East were they,
And they travelled by night and they slept by day,
  For their guide was a beautiful, wonderful star.

The star was so beautiful, large and clear,
  That all the other stars of the sky
Became a white mist in the atmosphere;
And by this they knew that the coming was near
  Of the Prince foretold in the prophecy.

Three caskets they bore on their saddle-bows,
  Three caskets of gold with golden keys;
Their robes were of crimson silk, with rows
Of bells and pomegranates and furbelows,
  Their turbans like blossoming almond-trees.

And so the Three Kings rode into the West,
  Through the dusk of night, over hill and dell,
And sometimes they nodded with beard on breast,
And sometimes talked, as they paused to rest,
  With the people they met at some wayside well.

"Of the child that is born," said Baltasar,
  "Good people, I pray you, tell us the news,
For we in the East have seen his star,
And have ridden fast, and have ridden far,
  To find and worship the King of the Jews."

And the people answered, "You ask in vain;
  We know of no king but Herod the Great!"
They thought the Wise Men were men insane,
As they spurred their horses across the plain
  Like riders in haste, and who cannot wait.

And when they came to Jerusalem,
  Herod the Great, who had heard this thing,
Sent for the Wise Men and questioned them;
And said, "Go down unto Bethlehem,
  And bring me tidings of this new king."

So they rode away, and the star stood still,
  The only one in the gray of morn;
Yes, it stopped,—it stood still of its own free will,
Right over Bethlehem on the hill,
  The city of David, where Christ was born.

And the Three Kings rode through the gate and the
      guard,
  Through the silent street, till their horses turned
And neighed as they entered the great inn-yard;
But the windows were closed, and the doors were barred,
  And only a light in the stable burned.

And cradled there in the scented hay,
  In the air made sweet by the breath of kine,
The little child in the manger lay,
The Child that would be King one day
  Of a kingdom not human, but divine.

His mother, Mary of Nazareth,
  Sat watching beside his place of rest,
Watching the even flow of his breath,
For the joy of life and the terror of death
  Were mingled together in her breast.

They laid their offerings at his feet:
  The gold was their tribute to a King;
The frankincense, with its odor sweet,
Was for the Priest, the Paraclete;
  The myrrh for the body's burying.

And the mother wondered and bowed her head,
  And sat as still as a statue of stone;
Her heart was troubled yet comforted,
Remembering what the Angel had said
  Of an endless reign and of David's throne.

Then the Kings rode out of the city gate,
  With a clatter of hoofs in proud array;
For they went not back to Herod the Great,
For they knew his malice and feared his hate,
  And returned to their homes by another way.

*Henry Wadsworth Longfellow*

# Ballad of the Epiphany

When Christ was born in Bethlehem,
   Pan left his Sussex Downs,
To see three kings go riding by,
   All in their robes and crowns;
And, as they went in royal state,
   Pan followed them, unseen,
Though tiny tufts of grass and flowers
   Showed where his feet had been.

And when to Bethlehem they came,
   Birds sang in every tree,
And Mary in the stable sat,
   With Jesus on her knee;
And while the oxen munched their hay,
   The kings with one accord
Placed gold and frankincense and myrrh
   Before their infant Lord.

And when Pan peeped upon the scene,
   The Christ-Child clapped His hands,
And chuckled with delight to see
   The god of pasture lands;
And Mary sang *"Magnificat"*
   Above the kneeling kings,

And angels circled overhead
   On rainbow-colored wings.

And many a little singing bird
   Flew past the open door
To hop and chirrup in the straw
   Above the stable floor;
Wrens, robins, linnets, greenfinches,
   And many another one,
Flew in to show good fellowship
   With Mary's newborn Son.

Then Pan stood up and played his pipes
   Beside the manger-bed,
And every little bird went near
   And raised its faithful head;
And one, most beautiful to see,
   A fair and milk-white dove,
Arose and hovered in the air
   To testify its love.

But when the kings looked up to find
   Who made the piping sound,
They only saw white lilies shine,
   Fresh-gathered, on the ground,
And through the doorway, and beyond,
   A shaggy wild goat leap;
And, in its gentle mother's arm,
   The Baby fast asleep.

*Charles Dalmon*

# Babushka

**A RUSSIAN LEGEND**

Babushka sits before the fire
Upon a winter's night;
The driving winds heap up the snow,
Her hut is snug and tight;
The howling winds,—they only make
Babushka's fire more bright!

She hears a knocking at the door:
So late—who can it be?
She hastes to lift the wooden latch,
No thought of fear has she;
The wind-blown candle in her hand
Shines out on strangers three.

Their beards are white with age, and snow
That in the darkness flies;
Their floating locks are long and white,
But kindly are their eyes
That sparkle underneath their brows,
Like stars in frosty skies.

"Babushka, we have come from far,
We tarry but to say,

A little Prince is born this night,
Who all the world shall sway.
Come join the search; come, go with us,
Who go our gifts to pay."

Babushka shivers at the door;
"I would I might behold
The little Prince who shall be King
But ah! the night is cold,
The wind so fierce, the snow so deep,
And I, good sirs, am old."

The strangers three, no word they speak,
But fade in snowy space!
Babushka sits before her fire,
And dreams, with wistful face:
"I would that I had questioned them,
So I the way might trace!

"When morning comes with blessed light,
I'll early be awake;
My staff in hand I'll go,—perchance,
Those strangers I'll o'ertake;
And, for the Child some little toys
I'll carry, for His sake."

The morning came, and, staff in hand,
She wandered in the snow,
She asked the way of all she met,
But none the way could show.
"It must be farther yet," she sighed;
"Then farther will I go."

And still, 'tis said, on Christmas Eve,
When high the drifts are piled,
With staff, with basket on her arm,
Babushka seeks the Child:
At every door her face is seen,—
Her wistful face and mild!

Her gifts at every door she leaves;
She bends, and murmurs low,
Above each little face half-hid
By pillows white as snow:
"And is He here?" Then, softly sighs,
"Nay, farther must I go."

*Edith M. Thomas*

# Ballad of the Golden Bowl

"What is this golden bowl, mother,
With its strange design?
It is not like our other things,
But foreign, and fine . . ."

"It came out of the east, child,
Long, long ago.
Your grandmother gave it to us.
This is all we know:

When your father's brother was born
On a winter's night,
A new star stood in the skies.
It was a great sight—

And three kings rode from afar
To kneel at his bed.
They were seeking a greater King,
Or so they said . . ."

"And was he a king, mother?
My father's kin?"
"No, child, it was all a mistake;
It must have been—

For they went away, those three,
And they came no more.
And he had a sad life, child,
He died poor . . ."

"Had he a wife, mother,
And a boy of his own?"
"He had neither chick nor child, darling,
He was all alone.

He was a good man,
But he came to grief;
And they hanged him on a cross
Like a common thief."

"But why, mother, why,
If he was kind and good?"
"It was a plot of some sort, child,
We never understood.

There was nothing we could do,
Being humble folk.
He was your grandmother's favorite—
Her heart broke.

She gave us this golden bowl,
When she came to die.
It is sad—it is all we have
To remember him by . . ."

*Sara Henderson Hay*

# Indexes

# INDEX OF AUTHORS

## INDEX OF TITLES

# INDEX OF FIRST LINES

4791003 8
PN 6110 .C4 P27
PARKER ELINOR MILNO
100 MORE STORY POEMS

## DATE DUE

G79-10038
PARKER, ELINOR MILNOR

100 MORE STORY POEMS

## MONTGOMERY COLLEGE
## LIBRARY
## GERMANTOWN CAMPUS

G79-10038
PN
6110
.C4
P27

DEMCO